The Intuitive Arts
on
WORK

The Intuitive Arts

on

WORK

Arlene Tognetti and Deborah S. Romaine

ALPHA

A member of Penguin Group (USA) Inc.

International Standard Book Number: 1-59257-108-5
Library of Congress Catalog Card Number: 2003108344

05   04   03   8   7   6   5   4   3   2   1

Interpretation of the printing code: The rightmost number of the first series of numbers is the year of the book's printing; the rightmost number of the second series of numbers is the number of the book's printing. For example, a printing code of 03-1 shows that the first printing occurred in 2003.

Printed in the United States of America

Publisher: Marie Butler-Knight
Product Manager: Phil Kitchel
Senior Managing Editor: Jennifer Chisholm
Senior Acquisitions Editor: Randy Ladenheim-Gil
Book Producer: Lee Ann Chearney/Amaranth Illuminare
Development Editor: Lynn Northrup
Copy Editor: Keith Cline
Technical Editor: Reba Jean Cain
Cover Designer: Charis Santillie
Book Designer: Trina Wurst
Creative Director: Robin Lasek
Layout/Proofreading: Angela Calvert, John Etchison

Contents

Appendixes

Introduction

Claim your brightest destiny and fulfill your own essential nature.

More than ever, we are searching for an inner awareness that brings outer confidence, joy, and direction. *The Intuitive Arts* series, with volumes on Work, Family, Health, Love, and Money, gives readers looking for answers to questions of daily living tools from the esoteric arts that will help them look deeply, see, and make real changes affecting their futures. Curious querents are presented in each problem-solving volume with exercises in the Intuitive Arts of Astrology, Tarot, and Psychic Intuition that examine, instruct, illuminate, and guide. In essence, you get three books for one—but also so much more!

An understanding of the interplay of the Intuitive Arts of Astrology, Tarot, and Psychic Intuition is something most people gain slowly over time, or with the aid of a professional Intuitive Arts practitioner who already has the knowledge to give in-depth readings that link the arts together.

In *The Intuitive Arts* series, expert author Arlene Tognetti shares her deep knowing of the arts of Astrology, Tarot, and Psychic Intuition to give you the best opportunity to work out solutions to life's problems and challenges with the benefit of the sophisticated relationships between the arts Arlene reveals chapter by chapter. By combining the Intuitive Arts together throughout each chapter's exercises, you'll gain insights that link the arts together—how, for example, the Tarot's Elemental reactions deepen insights into your astrological Workplace Elemental Essence. Or what Psychic Intuition reveals about how Astrology's ascendant, or rising sign, directs the first impression you make at work, while your astrological midheaven guides you on a path of life-work and learning.

Arlene Tognetti and New Age book producer Lee Ann Chearney at Amaranth Illuminare created this series for Alpha Books to respond to the public's growing fascination with all things spiritual. People (like you!) want to know how they can use the Intuitive Arts to solve everyday challenges, plan for the future, and live in the present, with hands-on advice and techniques that will make things better for them. We want to help you improve the issues surrounding your unique life situation by providing a multi-art approach that gives you multiple pathways to personal growth and answers your questions about work, family, health, love, and money.

Using Tarot's Major and Minor Arcana cards and spreads; Astrology's birth charts and aspect grids, sign, planets, and houses; and Psychic Intuition's meditations, affirmations, and inner knowing exercises—the innovative *Intuitive Arts* series provides a truly interactive, solution-oriented, positive message that enriches a personal synergy of mind, body, and spirit!

Read on to further your knowledge and understanding of how the Intuitive Arts work together to reveal deep insights. In this series volume, *The Intuitive Arts on Work,* learn how Astrology, the Tarot, and Psychic Intuition reveal your future lifework!

Are *you* ready for success?

chapter 1

Success Is Your Work of Art

The metaphor of the Fool
Are you having a career crisis?
Astrology reveals the *real* you
Psychic Intuition and your inner senses
Tarot and the stories of your lifework
What do you want in your work?

Although work isn't (and shouldn't be) everything in your life, it is a cornerstone of your life's foundation ... and it's one of the three main reasons people consult astrologers like Arlene. (The other two reasons are money and relationships.) Arlene tells her clients, "You want to be happy and satisfied in life? Be happy and satisfied in your work!" Are you finding that easier said than done? Maybe it's time to let the Intuitive Arts—Astrology, Psychic Intuition, and Tarot—help you understand your interests, talents, and challenges so you can find your career path to lifework filled with happiness and satisfaction.

It's the Fool's Journey!

The first card of the Tarot, the Fool, is a metaphor for beginnings and opportunities. The Fool symbolizes enthusiasm, optimism, hope, and the courage of the innocent. With golden boots, white rose in hand (the classic symbol of transformation), and a satchel embossed with wings, the Fool sets off on the adventure of a lifetime. It doesn't matter where the Fool has been; the focus is on the journey ahead. There are always risks, like the cliff the Fool appears about ready to walk right off. But there's the little dog to sound a warning, and we can't really see how far down the Fool might fall ... if at all. This is the joy of the Fool's journey.

The "0" number of the Fool is the universal metaphor for endless-ness. It is the circle with no beginning and no end, the perpetual path. Where does the Fool's path go? Who knows! Not the Fool, and not you. You don't know where your path leads until you follow it. And you can't just stand there, looking at it, trying to see where it goes. You must dare to step forward, to walk the path, to create your way in the world. When it comes to the Fool's journey, opportunities are as end-less as the path itself.

Yes, there are risks. There are always challenges, hazards, dangers—cliffs. Your mission is to become aware, informed, and intentful in your travels. And as you take the Fool's journey through this book, that will happen! When you follow the Fool, the World is yours.

The Tarot's Major Arcana card the Fool leads the way to career satisfaction and success ... to the World.

Like the Fool, you can pack light for your Intuitive Arts journey ... most of what you need you already have within you. In this book, we use the Intuitive Arts of Psychic Intuition, the Tarot, and Astrology to explore your career path and its many options. Although we ask you to write down your responses and perceptions right here in this book for many of the exercises, we suggest that you also create an Intuitive Arts Journal. You can buy a blank book or bound journal for this, if you like, or just use a three-ring binder into which you can insert pages with your notes and comments. You'll want to record your Psychic Intuition insights, your Tarot spreads and interpretations of them, and the understandings that come to you as you learn more about Astrology.

☙ Your **Psychic Intuition**—your inner vision—is your inner Fool, your guide on the path to your lifework. You probably use this

Intuitive Art so often you aren't even aware, from those "gut" responses that direct you to make a left turn instead of a right and later you find out guided you around a major traffic snarl to the "instinct" that guides you to approach a new client just when that client is looking for your services. Your Psychic Intuition focuses, shapes, and interprets the information that comes to you through your daily life and through the other Intuitive Arts.

☙ The foundation of **Astrology** is your birth chart, a "Kodak moment" of the heavens at the moment of your first breath. Your birth chart is the blueprint of your life, showing the influences of planetary energies as they affect your interests, talents, and challenges throughout your life. You can follow along throughout the book using the example birth charts we use, but you'll want your personal birth chart so you can apply what you learn to your own life and career decisions.

Arlene used the computer software program Solar Fire 5 published by Astrolabe, Inc. to generate the birth charts we've adapted as examples throughout this book. Charts are cast using the Geocentric view, Tropical zodiac, Placidus house system, and True Node because these are the most common in modern Western Astrology. To get a birth chart that you can use with this book, be sure to specify these parameters. You can obtain just your birth chart (without interpretation) for a nominal cost from an astrologer, through metaphysical bookstores, and through Internet websites. Appendix A provides more detailed information.

☙ The **Tarot** as an Intuitive Art dates to medieval times when mystics hand-created decks of varying counts. The modern Tarot deck, which came into use in the late 1800s, contains 78 cards of consistent (although broadly interpreted across different deck designs) symbolic images. You can buy a deck of Tarot cards in metaphysical stores and many bookstores. You'll find that there are hundreds of designs; feel free to choose whatever one appeals to you. In this book, we use the Universal Waite Tarot Deck published by U.S. Games Systems, Inc. Appendix B contains images of the Tarot cards in this deck and brief descriptions of their general meanings.

Are you ready now to follow the Fool, stepping boldly onto the path of your future? This is *your* journey to success and bliss in your career, your lifework, and beyond!

The Quest for Career Satisfaction

The U.S. Department of Labor's Bureau of Labor Statistics reports that between the ages of 18 and 36, the typical American holds 10 jobs. Not surprisingly, we change jobs most frequently when we're younger—that's when we're learning the scope of our interests and the lay of the occupational landscape. But throughout our working lives, only 20 percent of us stay with the same employer for 5 years or longer. If you're feeling the itch to move on in your career, you're certainly not alone.

Many people are looking for new opportunities because they're not satisfied, happy, or fulfilled in their current jobs. The problem is, they keep ending up in the same kinds of situations because they don't know *why* they're not satisfied, happy, or fulfilled. We have plenty of examples and exercises throughout this book that show you how the Intuitive Arts can help you identify and understand your talents, abilities, interests, needs and challenges—in short, to find *your* path to happiness and satisfaction in your job and your career.

Who Are You? Heaven Knows!

At the precise moment of your birth, the planetary bodies occupied a particular alignment in the heavens, or Zodiac. Your first breath etched that alignment into a representation of your life's blueprint—your birth chart. A planet's position at the moment of your birth imbues you with its energy, which helps to define who you are and explain why you are the way you are.

The Zodiac is a circular representation of the heavens, divided into 12 equal sections. We know these as the 12 signs of the Zodiac. Each sign of the Zodiac represents a location in the sky and symbolizes particular characteristics. Each sign also has a ruling planet (some signs have two rulers) that focuses the sign's energy.

Astro Sign	Key Characteristics	Ruling Planet(s)
Aries ♈	Independent, competitive, physical	Mars ♂
Taurus ♉	Persistent, loyal, stable	Venus ♀
Gemini ♊	Curious, objective, intellectual	Mercury ☿
Cancer ♋	Nurturing, protective, emotional	Moon ☽
Leo ♌	Strong, dynamic, creative	Sun ☉
Virgo ♍	Practical, dependable, precise	Mercury ☿

Astro Sign	Key Characteristics	Ruling Planet(s)
Libra ♎	Patient, diplomatic, balanced	Venus ♀
Scorpio ♏	Passionate, resilient, determined	Mars ♂ and Pluto ♇
Sagittarius ♐	Enthusiastic, generous, open-minded	Jupiter ♃
Capricorn ♑	Pragmatic, efficient, diligent	Saturn ♄
Aquarius ♒	Idealistic, inventive, selfless	Saturn ♄ and Uranus ♅
Pisces ♓	Visionary, compassionate, intuitive	Jupiter ♃ and Neptune ♆

The wheel of houses is a symbolic presentation, also circular and divided into 12 sections, of the Zodiac and its areas of influence. The lines that separate the houses are called cusps; they mark the end of one house and the start of another. Each house has a natural sign and affiliated planetary ruler that directs the house's influences. Each house accounts for an area of your life, just as each room in the house where you live accommodates a particular function.

Astro House	Areas of Life	Natural Astro Sign	Natural Astro Ruler(s)
1st house of self	Identity, self, persona, the body, physical appearance	Aries ♈	Mars ♂, Pluto ♇
2nd house of values	Resources, money, possessions, ability to earn	Taurus ♉	Venus ♀
3rd house of communication	Knowledge, public speaking, writing, the media	Gemini ♊	Mercury ☿
4th house of home	Family, home, real estate, sense of personal security, foundations	Cancer ♋	Moon ☽
5th house of creativity	Self-expression, creativity, children	Leo ♌	Sun ☉
6th house of work	Routine work habits, service, job activities	Virgo ♍	Mercury ☿

Astro House	Areas of Life	Natural Astro Sign	Natural Astro Ruler(s)
7th house of partnerships	One-to-one relation-ships, business partnerships, marriage	Libra ♎	Venus ♀
8th house of transformations	Change, transition, transformation, others' resources and money, inheritance, intimacy	Scorpio ♏	Mars ♂, Pluto ♀
9th house of philosophy	Beliefs, philosophical foundations, truth, higher knowledge and education, publishing	Sagittarius ♐	Jupiter ♃
10th house of career	Career reputation, achievement, pro-fessional recognition	Capricorn ♑	Saturn ♄
11th house of humanitarianism	Life goals, friends, humanitarianism, the greater good	Aquarius ♒	Uranus ♅, Saturn ♄
12th house of secrets	Inner self, spiritual self, mysticism, secrets, hidden agendas	Pisces ♓	Neptune ♆, Jupiter ♃

Before you move in—before your birth—the wheel of houses exists as a natural, neutral structure. When you arrive on the scene, the place-ment of your planets and their signs personalizes the wheel and it becomes your unique birth chart. It's sort of like moving into a real house—the house's structure is there, with its walls and rooms and other natural characteristics. When you move in, you might paint the walls, hang pictures, put all your furniture in place. From the outside it might look like every other house built from the same set of plans, but on the inside it's uniquely *your* house.

The planets, in Astrology, include the Sun ☉ and the Moon ☽ (called the luminaries) as well as the other 8 planets of our solar system. (Astrology doesn't incorporate our home planet Earth as a planetary influence.) Each planet's name is that of a mythological god or goddess, reflecting the planet's energy and characteristics. Each planet has a natu-ral sign, the sign in which it symbolically resides and that it rules. Some planets rule more than one sign and house.

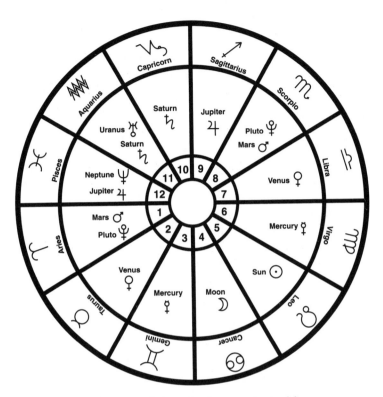

The natural planets and signs in the astrological houses.

Planet	Planet's Focus	Rules the Sign(s)	Rules the House(s)
Sun ☉	Self, potential	Leo ♌	5th house of creativity
Moon ☽	Emotions, intuition	Cancer ♋	4th house of home
Mercury ☿	Communication	Gemini ♊, Virgo ♍	3rd house of communication, 6th house of work
Venus ♀	Money, art, beauty	Taurus ♉, Libra ♎	2nd house of values, 7th house of partnerships
Mars ♂	Personal power	Aries ♈, Scorpio ♏	1st house of self, 8th house of transformations
Jupiter ♃	Fortune, good luck	Sagittarius ♐, Pisces ♓	9th house of philosophy, 12th house of secrets

Planet	Planet's Focus	Rules the Sign(s)	Rules the House(s)
Saturn ♄	Structure, learning, discipline	Capricorn ♑, Aquarius ♒	10th house of career, 11th house of humanitarianism
Uranus ♅	Originality, radical change	Aquarius ♒	11th house of humanitarianism
Neptune ♆	Mysticism, idealism	Pisces ♓	12th house of secrets
Pluto ♀	Rebirth, regeneration	Scorpio ♏	8th house of transformation

As each planet travels the path of its orbit, it moves through—as astrologers say, transits—the other signs of the Zodiac. One completion of its orbit takes a planet through all of the signs; the length of time the planet spends in each sign depends on the length and nature of the planet's orbit.

Your Personal Signs

When you're born, the signs symbolizing the planetary placements in the heavens at the moment of your birth take up representative stations along the cusps of your birth chart's wheel of houses. Their planetary rulers then direct how the energies of the planets within the houses affect the respective areas of your life.

Three cusp signs have special significance for your job and career:

- ☙ Your **ascendant**, which is on the cusp between the 12th and 1st houses and influences the 1st house of self. Your ascendant (sometimes called your rising sign) represents your public persona—how you present yourself to people who don't know you.

- ☙ Your **descendant** is opposite your ascendant, along a line aptly called your chart's horizon. On the cusp between the 6th and 7th houses, your descendant is the sign that influences the 7th house, the house of partnerships. Your descendant represents how you approach one-to-one relationships like business partnerships and working relationships with your co-workers.

- ☙ Your **midheaven** is on the cusp separating the 9th and 10th houses and influences the 10th house of career. The sign of your midheaven identifies the way others perceive you through your work and career.

Your Birth Chart

Your birth chart shows the 12 houses with symbols that represent the planets and the signs they occupied (showing their positions in the Zodiac) at the time of your birth. One house might be crowded with planets and another vacant. From their positions, the planets focus the energies of the signs they rule; those signs in turn influence how you perceive and function in the areas of your life that correlate to the houses in which they reside. Two of your birth chart's houses, the 6th and the 10th, represent your work and your career path.

Your 2nd house of values is also important when looking at your job and career. Your 2nd house reflects the talents and abilities—your personal resources—that you bring to your work as well as your capacity to earn income through them. The sign on the cusp of your 2nd house and the planets that reside in your 2nd house show what those talents and abilities might include and tell how you might use them in the context of work.

The relationships between planets form energy paths called aspects. Aspects can be favorable, in which case they support and facilitate the flow of energy between the planets. Or they can be challenging, presenting a struggle between opposing forces. Some aspects are conditional; whether they are favorable or challenging depends on the aligned planets. Many birth charts also include a triangular grid called an aspect grid that shows a summary the aspects. We'll show you Bruce Springsteen's birth chart and aspect grid later as an example.

We identify Bruce's personal signs and planets, so you can see how to find them, and associate them with their key characteristics. In later chapters, we have you do this with your own birth chart.

Bruce's	Astro Sign	Influence	Key Characteristics
Ascendant in (*1st house cusp*)	Gemini ♊	Presents self to others as	Curious, objective, intellectual
Descendant in (*7th house cusp*)	Sagittarius ♐	Approaches relationships as	Enthusiastic, generous, open-minded
Midheaven in (*10th house cusp*)	Aquarius ♒	Others perceive through work as	Idealistic, inventive, selfless

Bruce's Planets	Astro Sign	Key Characteristics	Astro House/Area
Sun ☉ in *planet of self and potential*	Libra ♎	Is patient, diplomatic, balanced	4th house of home
Moon ☽ in *planet of emotions and intuition*	Libra ♎	Is patient, diplomatic, balanced	5th house of creativity
Mercury ☿ in *planet of communication*	Libra ♎	Is patient, diplomatic, balanced	5th house of creativity
Venus ♀ in *planet of money, art, beauty*	Scorpio ♏	Is passionate, resilient, determined	5th house of creativity
Mars ♂ in *planet of personal power*	Leo ♌	Is strong, dynamic, creative	3rd house of communication
Jupiter ♃ in *planet of fortune*	Capricorn ♑	Is pragmatic, efficient, diligent	8th house of transformation
Saturn ♄ in *planet of structure, learning, discipline*	Virgo ♍	Is practical, dependable, precise	4th house of home
Uranus ♅ in *planet of originality, radical change*	Cancer ♋	Is nurturing, protective, emotional	1st house of self
Neptune ♆ in *planet of mysticism, idealism*	Libra ♎	Is patient, diplomatic, balanced	5th house of creativity
Pluto ♇ in *planet of regeneration*	Leo ♌	Is strong, dynamic, creative	3rd house of communication

If you have your birth chart, you can look at it to see what you can identify about your signs, planets, and houses. Can you locate your Sun ☉ sign and your Moon ☽ sign? Don't worry if it all seems like hieroglyphics right now! In the following chapters, we guide you through the information your birth chart contains.

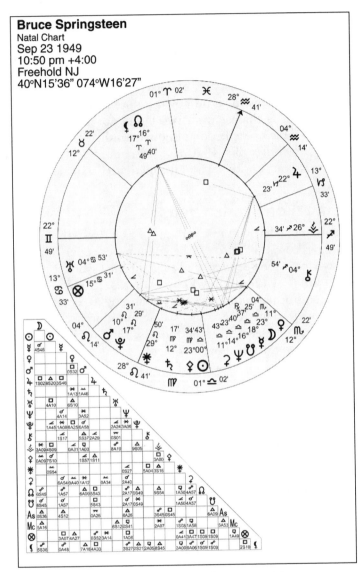

Bruce Springsteen
Natal Chart
Sep 23 1949
10:50 pm +4:00
Freehold NJ
40°N15'36" 074°W16'27"

Bruce Springsteen's birth chart with aspect grid.

Noon Birth Charts

An astrologer needs the date, time, and place (city and state) of your birth to cast your birth chart. Most people born in the United States and on most American military installations can find this information on their birth certificates. If you don't have access to your birth certificate, a relative or family friend might remember whether you were born in the morning or at night, to help narrow the window.

If all you have is the date and place of your birth, an astrologer can cast a birth chart that uses noon as your time of birth. With a noon birth chart, your ascendant, descendant, midheaven, and Moon ☽ sign may or may not be accurate depending on how far your true birth time is from noon. Ascendant signs change every two hours, for example. There are circumstances in which people don't know even their true birth dates and locations; sometimes this is the case with adoptions. If this is your situation, discuss your options with an experienced astrologer.

Activating Your Inner Senses

Psychic Intuition is what you might think of as your sixth sense. Your analytical, logical brain likes to put perceptions, experiences, memories, and thoughts where they're *supposed to* go. Your Psychic Intuition doesn't know *supposed to*; it only knows what *is*. Psychic Intuition lets you experience information in ways not bound by expectations or conventions. One way to broaden your Psychic Intuition is to practice this kind of experiencing. Here's a simple exercise that, once you get the knack of it, you can do any time, any place.

We start with the physical sense of vision. First, pick a color, any color. Write it here:

I choose the color _____.

What is your visual experience of the color? What do you see when you look at this color? Write your response here:

I visualize the color _____ as _____.

Now turn your experience of the color over to your Psychic Intuition. What is the first perception you have about the color? It doesn't matter how you express this perception. Write it here:

My Psychic Intuition perceives the color _____ as

_____.

Let your Psychic Intuition perceive the color as a sound, taste, smell, and touch. Don't think about your responses; your analytical brain has to sit this one out. Write your perceptions here:

The color _____ sounds like _____.

The color _____ tastes like _____.

The color _____ smells like _____.

The color _____ feels like _____.

Although you now have different and unexpected experiences of the color red, your base perception remains pretty much the same. You simply perceive *more* about red than you're accustomed to perceiving!

Let your Psychic Intuition explore the experiences of your other physical senses in similar fashion—choose items to represent hearing, taste, smell, and touch. This exercise helps you to accept the input of your Psychic Intuition.

Reading the Cards

If all the workplace is a stage, then the Tarot is its cast of characters. These metaphorical images can represent people, places, events—just about any circumstance in your life (past, present, and future). Tarot cards, like Astrology, project possibilities and reveal insights. Their symbolic, representative nature gives you great latitude for interpreting their meanings. These images, like the houses, planets, and signs of Astrology, represent certain archetypes or universal concepts arising from ancient mythology. Although Tarot incorporates specific ways of reading the cards, called spreads, interpretations are highly intuitive and subjective.

There are two major divisions of cards, the Major Arcana (22 cards) and the Minor Arcana (56 cards). The Minor Arcana consist of 4 suits with 14 cards each, and each suit containing 4 royalty cards and 10 numbered cards. Major Arcana cards represent themes in your life; Minor Arcana cards represent the everyday details of carrying out those themes.

The Tarot's 22 Major Arcana cards correspond to the 12 signs of the Zodiac; all the astrological signs except Gemini Ⅱ and Sagittarius ♐ have 2 or more Tarot card affiliations.

Astro Sign	Major Arcana Tarot Cards
Aries ♈	The Fool, the Magician, the Emperor
Taurus ♉	The Empress, the Hierophant, the Wheel of Fortune
Gemini Ⅱ	The Lovers
Cancer ♋	Temperance, the Moon
Leo ♌	Strength, the Wheel of Fortune, the Sun

Astro Sign	Major Arcana Tarot Cards
Virgo ♍	The High Priestess, the Hermit
Libra ♎	The Empress, Justice
Scorpio ♏	The Emperor, the Wheel of Fortune, Death, Judgement
Sagittarius ♐	The Chariot
Capricorn ♑	The Devil, the World
Aquarius ♒	The Wheel of Fortune, the Tower, the Star
Pisces ♓	The High Priestess, the Hanged Man, the Moon

THE EMPEROR.   WHEEL of FORTUNE.   DEATH.   JUDGEMENT.

The Tarot's Major Arcana cards correspond to the astrological signs. The Emperor, the Wheel of Fortune, Death, and Judgement, for example, all correspond to the sign of Scorpio ♏.

All the Tarot cards can offer insights into your questions and issues related to work and career. These Major Arcana cards have particular significance:

- ☯ The World—success
- ☯ The Lovers—partnerships
- ☯ The Emperor—leadership
- ☯ The Empress—prosperity

Find these four cards in your Tarot deck—the World, the Sun, the Emperor, and the Empress—and lay them on the table in front of you. (Or you can look at the illustrations of them here, although you'll have to use the inner vision of your Psychic Intuition to supply the colors and other details that only the cards themselves can display.) Which one of the four cards do you feel represents your feelings about work *right now?* What do you feel when you look at this card? Resist the temptation to "think" the card's imagery; instead, let your Psychic Intuition guide your responses.

The Tarot's Major Arcana card the World represents success, the Lovers represents partnerships, the Emperor represents leadership, and the Empress represents prosperity.

Card that most represents my feelings about work:

_____.

_____.

Perceptions and feelings this card evokes:

_____.

Like the houses of Astrology, the Tarot's Minor Arcana suits represent areas of life. Each suit also corresponds to four of the astrological signs.

Minor Arcana Suit	Area of Life	Astro Signs
Wands	Work	Aries ♈, Leo ♌, Sagittarius ♐
Swords	Personal power	Gemini ♊, Libra ♎, Aquarius ♒
Pentacles	Resources, money	Taurus ♉, Virgo ♍, Capricorn ♑
Cups	Relationships	Cancer ♋, Scorpio ♏, Pisces ♓

Within the four suits of the Minor Arcana cards, the court cards—King, Queen, Knight, Page—often correspond to specific or representative people. Let's take a look at the court cards for the suit of work, Wands.

The court cards of the Tarot's Minor Arcana suit of Wands.

There's the King of Wands, confident in his role as leader. He wears his regal robes and adornments comfortably, almost casually, displaying his accomplishments and successes as well as his openness to new ideas and adventures. He holds the staff of his personal power—his talents and skills—in his right hand, upright and proud. The chameleon at his side symbolizes his capacity for change, his ability to "go with the flow" when necessary.

The Queen of Wands looks quite regal, too, with her rich yellow robes and substantial crown. With equal pride she holds the staff of her talents in her right hand and the "harvest" of her labors in the other. Look at the pair of lions on the throne behind her head ... here is a leader who believes strength and success come through collaboration.

In the Tarot, Knights represent action. The Knight of Wands launches into his next adventure with enthusiasm and intensity, not quite sure where his journey is leading him but certain of his ability to meet whatever challenges lie ahead. And Pages represent communication; they are the Tarot's messengers. What message does the Page of Wands bear? It seems good news.

When you explore the imagery of these court cards—the King, Queen, Knight, and Page of Wands—do people from your workplace come immediately to mind? Does the King or the Queen make you think of your boss or a business partner? In what ways? Do you see yourself in any of these cards? Without analyzing your reactions, write down some of your first perceptions.

King of Wands: _____

Queen of Wands: _____

Knight of Wands: _____

Page of Wands: _____

Court cards also represent a condition or state of affairs that is bigger than your personal world. In such a context, the King of Wands might represent your company, if you work for a large corporation, the government, or collectively "The Man"—the powers that be, the holders of authority and control. The Knight of Wands, charging off on adventures unknown, might symbolize change and new direction within your industry.

The numbered cards of the Tarot's Minor Arcana often reflect people in relationship to events. Here the 3 of Cups suggests celebration, the 10 of Swords betrayal, and the 7 of Wands too much work, too little time.

The numbered cards of the Minor Arcana often bring to mind events. The exuberant celebration on the 3 of Cups, for example, might immediately evoke memories of your work team winning the company's productivity award last month or celebrating the successful launch of a new product line. Co-workers fail to support your proposal in the last staff meeting? The 10 of Swords might be just the card to reflect your feelings of betrayal! And what says, "How am I ever going to get all this work done by myself?" like the 7 of Wands?

The Tarot's numbered cards also suggest timing, both by number and by suit. By number, Ace through 10 represents 1 through 10 days, weeks, or months, depending on the suit.

Tarot Suit	Timing	Season
Wands	Weeks	Spring
Cups	Days	Summer
Swords	Hours or days	Fall
Pentacles	Months	Winter

A Simple Tarot Spread

The 3-Card Spread is one of the most popular Tarot readings because it's quick and easy. To do a 3-Card Spread, you need your Tarot deck. Shuffle it like you would any other deck of cards. While you're shuffling, ask the question, "What do I want in my work?" When you feel that you've shuffled the deck enough, divide it in any way you choose and pick out any three cards. Place them face up in front of you, left to right in the order you draw them. These three cards can represent what you feel *today* about what you're looking for in your work and career.

Card 1: _____

Card 2: _____

Card 3: _____

You might want to write some comments or notes in your Intuitive Arts Journal, and come back to this Tarot spread at a later time. It's only the beginning!

Success!

With this introduction to the Intuitive Arts of Astrology, Tarot, and Psychic Intuition, you're ready to set your Fool's foot on the path of your destiny—your unique and rewarding *lifework*. So with your astrological birth chart and Tarot deck in hand and your Psychic Intu-ition in mind and at heart, let's embark on the journey to manifest *your* success in life through the work you do.

chapter 2

The Yin and Yang of Home and Work Life

The contrasts and complement of *yin* and *yang*
Psychic Intuition finds the balance
Astrology's *yin/yang* balance profile
The astrological houses of home and work: 4th, 6th, 10th
Astrology's aspects: The influences of alignment
Tarot's *yin* and *yang* in the cards

Yin *and* yang, *the ancient Chinese duality, are the essential energies of existence—and of your life. When these two opposing energies thrive in equal share, there is balance. For many people, the challenge of balancing work and home can seem like a battle of opposing forces, a true dichotomy of competing interests. In balance, though, the* yin *and* yang *of work and home produce harmony. Your job description suits you and your work energizes you. Your career path is clear, and you enjoy where it's leading you. Your work supports a sense of satisfaction and security that extends to other areas of your life—home, family, relationships, health, and finances. Life is good. When you're unhappy and disgruntled in your job, when your work drains the enthusiasm right out of you, or you feel you have to give home life, your partner, or your children short shrift, your life feels out of balance. Instead of feeling boxed in,* The Intuitive Arts—Astrology, Tarot, *and* Psychic Intuition—*can help you restore the circle of* yin/yang *bliss.*

Yin and Yang: A Foundation of Complements

Too often we tend to view the world in terms of mutually exclusive opposites. When one force dominates, the other disappears—or at least so it seems. When you raise a cup of hot coffee to your lips, you notice the dominance of "hot," not the minimal presence of "cold." And of course, that's just how you want it—in your coffee cup! "Hot" and "cold," though, can be seen intuitively as polarities. They complement and complete each other, coming together to create balance and harmony. This is the essence of *yin* and *yang*, the basic foundations that create the flow of energy in the universe—and in your home life and your job or career, which together form your lifework.

These are some conventional characteristics of *yin* and *yang* balancing energies.

Yin	Yang
Feminine	Masculine
Cold	Hot
Soft	Hard
Receptive	Active
Under	Over
Moon	Sun
Nurture	Grow
Negative	Positive
Dark	Light
Intrinsic	Extrinsic

Which of these do you see in yourself? At home? In your job? In your workplace? In your co-workers? It's not that women are feminine and men are masculine. Each of us, woman or man, has both feminine and masculine energies. Nor is negative bad and positive good; rather, these reflect energy that leaves or enters, in the manner of electrical current.

As contrasts or as complements, *yin/yang* forces commonly exhibit a push and pull. *Yin* to *yin* or *yang* to *yang* often feels comfortable at first. You feel as if the energy is working easily toward common goals and in compatible ways. But *yin/yin* or *yang/yang* pairings and situations can become challenging, too. The like pairing that seemed so ideal at first grows unrelenting without counterbalance. All that overtime that's great on your paycheck infringes on other values, like time to spend with family and friends. The extra work is too much *yang* energy, and it creates distress through imbalance. You feel better only when the balance shifts to let more *yin* energy enter—you work less overtime, giving you more time for the other pleasures in your life. Sometimes, like pairings produce a sameness that grows routine and uninteresting, too *yang* hard-charging or too *yin* go with the flow.

As much as it reflects opposites and contrasts, the ancient Eastern yin/yang symbol also represents wholeness, completeness, fulfillment, and balance through harmonic union.

Here on the printed page, *yin* and *yang* exist in equilibrium. Can you find where one image ends and its complement starts? Not really! There is no more of one swirl than the other. The line that marks the end of one simultaneously marks the start of the other. Each image is in harmony with its counterpart, coexisting in balance.

Would that their energies did the same to balance your lifework! On paper, their symbolic existence is as static as it is perfect. In the real world, in the reality that is your life, *yin* and *yang* are dynamic. They shift around, sometimes with unexpected and astonishing force. Like magnets, their polarities push and pull the pieces of your life into, or out of, balance.

Where's Your Balance?

Surveys tell us that about two thirds of us are searching for balance between work and home. Many people feel they spend too much time at work, commuting to and from work, thinking about work—or, in what is becoming the status quo of the twenty-first century, bringing work home. Balance is not just about how much you work and whether you have enough time for the other parts of your life, though. Balance also is about how much you enjoy your work and the time you spend doing it, and whether you have time when you want or need it.

The 2 of Pentacles can't seem to get both feet on the ground as he juggles what he values while the waves toss around the ships of his fortune. The 10 of Pentacles appears to have it all, and all in balance—resources, family, security, comfort, and even a pair of smiling dogs!

What is the state of balance in *your* life? Every day this week, take this book and your Psychic Intuition to work. Three times each day, take three minutes to sit quietly in your workspace or someplace at work where you can safely close your eyes. Using your Psychic Intuition, create a portal that transports you to a parallel universe. This universe is every bit the same as the one you now inhabit, with one important difference: You live out the ideal balance of work and home. End each meditation session by writing down three intuitive strategies to make your ideal balance a real-world reality. Track the pattern of your responses in your Intuitive Arts notebook. Start here, now:

1. _____

2. _____

3. _____

Heavenly Polarities

According to ancient myth, *yin* and *yang* are the primal forces of the universe that came into being with the earth's birth. The opposing forces of these energies keep heaven and earth apart. They exist in balance to maintain equilibrium. The signs and houses of the Astrology's Zodiac also have energies that are *yin* or *yang*. Their energies support this balance in the universe and in your life.

Each of the 12 houses in your birth chart has a polarity, alternating *yin* and *yang* around the wheel. Houses directly across from each other have the same polarity, holding each other in balance. Six houses are *yin*, six are *yang*.

The Tarot's Major Arcana cards the Moon and the Sun symbolize the characteristics of yin *and* yang.

Yin Houses	**Yang Houses**
2nd house of values	1st house of self
4th house of home	3rd house of communication
6th house of work	5th house of creativity
8th house of transformation	7th house of partnerships
10th house of career	9th house of philosophy
12th house of secrets	11th house of humanitarianism

Notice any patterns? Yep—evens are *yin,* odds are *yang.* Notice anything else? Your houses of work (6th), career (10th), and home (4th) are all *yin.* Balance between these houses comes through the energies that reside *within* them—the signs and their ruling planets. Each of the 12 astrological signs of the Zodiac also has polarity, alternating in similar fashion to the houses.

Yin Astro Signs	**Yang Astro Signs**
Taurus ♉	Aries ♈
Cancer ♋	Gemini ♊
Virgo ♍	Leo ♌
Scorpio ♏	Libra ♎
Capricorn ♑	Sagittarius ♐
Pisces ♓	Aquarius ♒

Each house has a natural sign affiliation. In the natural order of things, this sign is the same energy—*yin* or *yang*—as the house. Aries ♈ naturally rules the 1st house, for example, and both the sign and the house are *yang.* Taurus ♉ naturally rules the 2nd house, and both are *yin.*

Your Yin/Yang Astrological Signature

In your astrological birth chart, though, which represents the planetary placements at the moment of *your* birth and how their energies influence your life, these affiliations might be different from the natural houses. You might have *yang* Leo ♌ on your *yin* 2nd house cusp, or *yin* Pisces ♓ on your 5th house cusp, setting up a bit of tension between the energies. Let's take a look at how this works in the noonchart of former New York mayor Rudy Giuliani. Notice that we highlighted the 4th, 6th, and 10th houses. These are your houses of home, work, and career, respectively; their signs are particularly important when it comes to how well personal energies match with work energies.

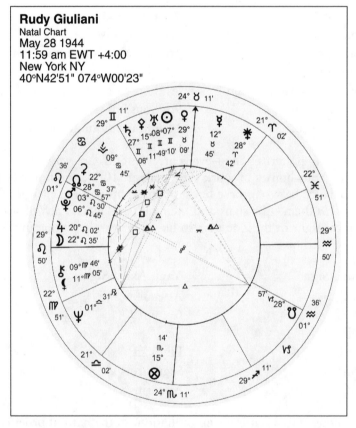

Former New York City mayor Rudy Giuliani's noon birth chart.

Astro House	House Polarity	Rudy's House Sign	Sign's Yin/ Yang Polarity
1st	*Yang*	Leo ♌	*Yang*
2nd	*Yin*	Virgo ♍	*Yin*
3rd	*Yang*	Libra ♎	*Yang*
4th	**Yin**	**Scorpio ♏**	**Yin**
5th	*Yang*	Sagittarius ♐	*Yang*
6th	**Yin**	**Aquarius ♒**	**Yang**
7th	*Yang*	Aquarius ♒	*Yang*
8th	*Yin*	Pisces ♓	*Yin*
9th	*Yang*	Aries ♈	*Yang*
10th	**Yin**	**Taurus ♉**	**Yin**
11th	*Yang*	Gemini ♊	*Yang*
12th	*Yin*	Leo ♌	*Yang*

With *yang* Aquarius ♒ on his *yin* 6th house of work, determination and originality rule Rudy's approach to his job. Such an overall *yang* personality needs the balance of his resilient, emotional *yin* Scorpio ♏ on his *yin* 4th house of home, and his dogged, faithful *yin* Taurus ♉ on his *yin* 10th house of career.

Okay, so what is *your* personal *yin/yang* astrological signature? Use your birth chart to complete the following table, as we did for Rudy Giuliani.

Astro House	House Polarity	Your House Sign	Sign's Yin/ Yang Polarity
1st	*Yang*	_____	_____
2nd	*Yin*	_____	_____
3rd	*Yang*	_____	_____
4th	**Yin**	_____	_____
5th	*Yang*	_____	_____
6th	**Yin**	_____	_____
7th	*Yang*	_____	_____
8th	*Yin*	_____	_____
9th	*Yang*	_____	_____

Astro House	House Polarity	Your House Sign	Sign's Yin/ Yang Polarity
10th	*Yin*	_____	_____
11th	*Yang*	_____	_____
12th	*Yin*	_____	_____

What do the signs and polarities your 4th house of home, 6th house of work, and 10th house of career reveal about *your* approach to balancing home and work? Do they match or oppose the natural *yin* or *yang* of these houses?

The Essential You in Balance with Your 4th, 6th, and 10th Houses

Let's look more closely at how the signs of your 4th house of home, 6th house of work, and 10th house of career relate to who you are as a person, how you behave, and whether your work creates the best balance for your personality and style. Astrologers look at these three houses when revealing matters related to work. These three houses show the big picture of your career (10th), the daily picture of your job (6th), and the balance of your home (4th).

We're going to add to these houses the astrological signs and *yin/yang* polarities corresponding to your Sun ☉, your Moon ☽, your ascendant or rising sign, and your descendant. Your Sun ☉ sign gives insight to your essential self and your Moon ☽ sign to your inner intuitive self. Your ascendant to the "you" that you show to the world and your descendant is the "inner" you for which you seek your perfect complement in the outer world. (For example, a flowing Pisces ♓ descendant might seek an action-oriented Sagittarius ♐ to balance it.) You identified these in Chapter 1. Write them in the following table, along with the astrological signs and polarities you discovered in your birth chart for your 4th, 6th, and 10th houses.

Your Astro Planet or House	Your Astro Sign	Astro Sign's Yin/Yang Polarity
Sun ☉	_____	_____
Moon ☽	_____	_____

Your Astro Planet or House	Your Astro Sign	Astro Sign's Yin/Yang Polarity
Ascendant	_____	_____
Descendant	_____	_____
4th house of home	_____	_____
6th house of work	_____	_____
10th house of career (midheaven)	_____	_____

Before you begin to analyze whether your work creates the most beneficial balance to your true self, let's look at the 4th, 6th, and 10th houses and their natural planetary rulers and astrological signs. Then we'll look at the personal astrological signs of Leonardo DiCaprio's, Sally Ride's, and former U.S. president Jimmy Carter's 4th, 6th, and 10th houses, and see how their work balances their true selves.

The Big Picture: Your 10th House of Career

The 10th house shows the course, or career path, that develops from the job of your 6th house and leads you toward your greater lifework. More than an accumulation of the jobs you've held throughout your life, the 10th house is a reflection of how those jobs fit together (or not, sometimes) in moving you toward fulfillment in work. Your 10th house also tells you the type of work or service that best suits your unique blend of abilities and planetary influences.

The 10th house's natural planetary ruler Saturn ♄ imposes structure and responsibility to shape the industrious organization of Capricorn ♑, the house of career's natural sign. Stray from the path and you're likely to feel Capricorn's persistent pull with sharp tugs from Saturn ♄ should you fail to get the message. This is the root of those vague feelings of uneasiness that a particular job isn't quite right or your work isn't what it should be.

Your personal 10th house sign, which also happens to be your all-important midheaven, shows how planetary influences play out in your career and shape your public reputation. Let's peek into the 10th house of talented young actor Leonardo DiCaprio for a little enlightenment on the path of his lifework.

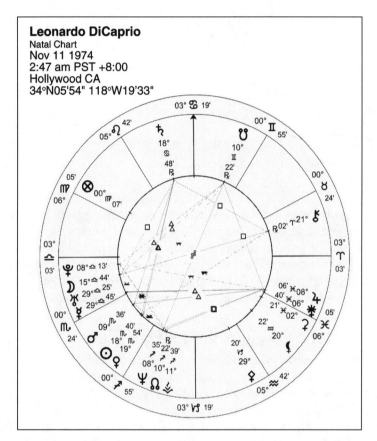

Leonardo DiCaprio's birth chart shows why this talented actor is a rising star.

With family-oriented Cancer ♋ ruling his 10th house of career, Leo always will need to feel what he is doing will benefit the family of those closest to him as well as the larger community. This is a flowing, *yin* energy—nurturing, intuitive, gentle. Although we see this actor in a range of roles from tender to harsh, he always brings his characters to life by drawing from this intrinsic *yin* source. Leo feels a strong emotional connection to his career and to the work that supports his path. Leo's *yin* Scorpio ♏ Sun shows that his core self, the essence of who he is, supports this expression of *yin* energy in his career. His Libra ♎ ascendant puts the drive of *yang* energy behind his efforts, balancing what could be a soft expression with bright, charging intensity. Yet he retreats again to the *yin* comfort of Capricorn ♑ on his 4th house of home.

Here's Leo's *yin/yang* polarity profile.

Astro Planet or House	Leo's Astro Sign	Leo's Yin/Yang Sign Polarity
Sun ☉	Scorpio ♏	*Yin*
Moon ☽	Libra ♎	*Yang*
Ascendant	Libra ♎	*Yang*
Descendant	Aries ♈	*Yang*
4th house of home	Capricorn ♑	*Yin*
6th house of work	Pisces ♓	*Yin*
10th house of career (midheaven)	Cancer ♋	*Yin*

Daily Details: Your 6th House of Work

As the 10th house gives the bigger picture of your career path, the 6th house tells the one-foot-in-front-of-the-other efforts you might follow to create that path. This is the house of daily duties (some might say daily grind), the actions you take day in and day out. The 6th house reflects how you approach your tasks: Are you organized and thorough? Do you step up to the plate when adversity throws a screwball, or look for someone else to take the hit? Are you 10 minutes early for everything, or do friends tease that your clocks have no hands?

The 6th house's natural *yin* ruler Virgo ♍ likes precision and detail, detail, detail. Virgo's virtuous energy drives perfectionism. Your personal astrological 6th house sign and its ruling planet can support this intense natural energy, or create challenges that show up in your life as habits that don't quite work for you, or a mismatch between your natural tendencies and the requirements of your job. The 6th house also embraces health. Your approach to the tasks of your job and to the tasks of your health and the fitness of your body typically are the same.

Let's take a look at the 6th house of high-flying physicist Sally Ride, the first American woman in space ... who went to college on a tennis scholarship. In 1977 Sally was one of 6 women and 29 men selected from among 8,000 applicants to join NASA's astronaut program. Six years later, she was a mission specialist aboard the space shuttle Challenger. Her key responsibility: testing the robotic arm she had helped to develop. Talk about reaching for the stars!

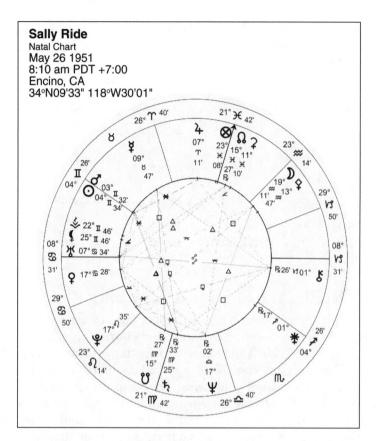

Sally Ride
Natal Chart
May 26 1951
8:10 am PDT +7:00
Encino, CA
34°N09'33" 118°W30'01"

*Former astronaut and first American woman in space Sally
Ride's chart shows a pioneering love of adventure riding
on an unwavering belief that all potential is attainable.*

Sagittarius ♐ rules Sally's 6th house of work and service to the
public, a driving *yang* energy able to push this woman's ambitions
through the challenges along her path. Sally's *yang* Gemini ♊ Sun ☉
and Aquarius ♒ Moon ☽ support this drive, while her *yin* Pisces ♓
midheaven helps her go with the flow and her *yin* Capricorn ♑ descendant pragmatically seeks the vision to stay fluid. Sally's *yin* Cancer ♋
ascendant, the face she shows to the world, tempers the potentially
confrontational nature of her determination.

Here's Sally's *yin/yang* polarity profile.

Astro Planet or House	Sally's Astro Sign	Sally's Yin/Yang Sign Polarity
Sun ☉	Gemini ♊	Yang
Moon ☽	Aquarius ♒	Yang
Ascendant	Cancer ♋	Yin
Descendant	Capricorn ♑	Yin
4th house of home	Virgo ♍	Yin
6th house of work	Sagittarius ♐	Yang
10th house of career (midheaven)	Pisces ♓	Yin

Comfort and Retreat: Your 4th House of Home

Home is where your roots are, the place you feel secure and grounded. Your 4th house of home tells what comforts you. It can represent your literal home—your place of family and domestic activity—as well as the figurative home for your sense of well-being. It speaks to your legacy—what you bring from your past (family history) and what you will shape from your life as you travel through it. The Moon ☽ is the 4th house's natural planetary ruler, shining her nurturing energy on the house of home's natural astrological sign of Cancer ♋. When the energies of your house of home are harmonious, you feel at peace with yourself and the world, safe and protected.

Former U.S. president Jimmy Carter managed to successfully blend a lifetime of public service with a strong family life. The clues to how he could do this are in his astrological birth chart. Jimmy's natal Sun ☉ in Libra ♎ shows that *yang* energy supports and drives his core being. His Libra ♎ ascendant reinforces this drive, integrating his essential self with his public persona. And we see ambitious, assertive, *yang* Aries ♈ ruling his 6th house of work. This is a man who enjoys competition … and often wins. Yet his *yang* Aries ♈ descendant seeks a balancing softness through partnerships.

Jimmy finds this softness in *yin* Cancer ♋ on his midheaven, showing the gentle diplomacy that's become the hallmark of this humanitarian. And on his 4th house, there's the *yin* of protective Capricorn ♑. Home is indeed a fortress for Jimmy Carter, holding the outside world at bay to create a safe and secure haven.

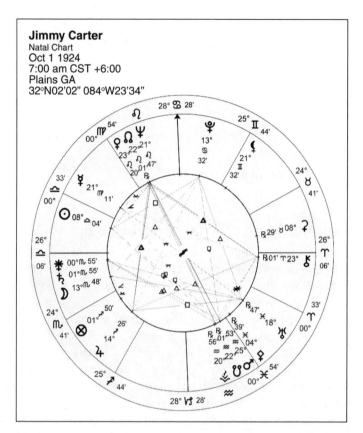

Jimmy Carter
Natal Chart
Oct 1 1924
7:00 am CST +6:00
Plains GA
32°N02'02" 084°W23'34"

Former U.S. president Jimmy Carter's birth chart shows a supportive yin/yang balance and flow of energy among his 4th, 6th, and 10th houses, including a wonderful grand trine △.

Here is Jimmy's *yin/yang* polarity profile.

Astro Planet or House	Jimmy's Astro Sign	Jimmy's Yin/Yang Sign Polarity
Sun ☉	Libra ♎	*Yang*
Moon ☽	Scorpio ♏	*Yin*
Ascendant	Libra ♎	*Yang*
Descendant	Aries ♈	*Yang*
4th house of home	Capricorn ♑	*Yin*
6th house of work	Aries ♈	*Yang*
10th house of career (midheaven)	Cancer ♋	*Yin*

Putting It All in Balance

Now that you've seen the influences of the 4th, 6th, and 10th houses in the personal life work balance of Leo, Sally, and Jimmy, let's return where we started, to the chart of Rudy Giuliani, and examine where Rudy is in (or out of!) balance.

With his Sun ☉, Moon ☽, ascendant, and 6th house of work all in *yang* signs, and *yin* signs ruling his 4th house of home and 10th house of career, Rudy finds much energy to fuel his lifework path! Rudy's *yang* Aquarius ♒ descendant further reinforces his intellectual drive and his need to find balance in a softer *yin* complement to complete his inner self. Rudy's *yang* predominance may seem to pull him out of balance, but maybe this is precisely the path Rudy has chosen for this life—and one that fulfills his lifework, and benefits society, this time around!

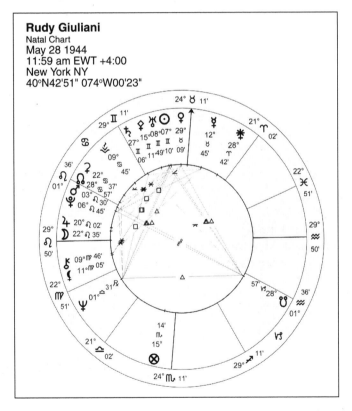

Rudy Giuliani's birth chart shows the public sector of his chart loaded with astrological energy, but not so much astrological support in his personal and private sectors.

Here's Rudy's *yin/yang* polarity profile.

Astro Planet or House	Rudy's Astro Sign	Rudy's Yin/Yang Sign Polarity
Sun ☉	Gemini ♊	*Yang*
Moon ☽	Leo ♌	*Yang*
Ascendant	Leo ♌	*Yang*
Descendant	Aquarius ♒	*Yang*
4th house of home	Scorpio ♏	*Yin*
6th house of work	Aquarius ♒	*Yang*
10th house of career (midheaven)	Taurus ♉	*Yin*

What does your astrological *yin/yang* balance profile say about you, your work, and your lifework?

Energies in Alignment: Aspects

Aspects are the relationships among the planets in your astrological birth chart. Aspects can be supportive and favorable, or confrontational and challenging. You can see the aspects in your birth chart as lines drawn across the center circle. There are squares, triangles, and other symbols on these lines that represent the aspect's nature. The lines connect the planets of the aspect.

You can also see the aspects in a grid, called an *aspectarian*. You can use either the aspect grid or the birth chart wheel to look at and interpret the aspects in your birth chart. For this exercise, we're going to use the chart wheel.

Astrologers analyze numerous aspects that have major and minor influences. There are five major aspects that you should know.

Astro Aspect	Symbol	Keywords
Conjunction	☌	Neutral; energies intensify each other; unpredictable
Sextile	✶	Opportunity or ability
Square	☐	Challenge or needs action
Trine	△	Flowing, smooth, easy
Opposition	☍	Out of balance

Aspects help you understand the flow of energy in your birth chart. If you think of aspects as streams of energy, trines △ and sextiles ✳ represent a smooth, harmonious flow. They're the most favorable aspects. Squares □ and oppositions ♂ signal turbulence and confrontation. They are the most challenging aspects. Conjunctions ♂ can support either harmony or challenge, depending on the planets.

Balancing Support and Challenge

Look back at Jimmy Carter's birth chart and you can see that he has many favorable aspects flowing from his 4th, 6th, and 10th houses that support his success in balancing and blending work and home. He also has what astrologers call a grand trine—an especially supportive configuration of multiple trines △ between planets. Can you find Jimmy's grand trine? It links his 2nd, 6th, and 10th houses, representing his desire to protect and keep balance in life. The balance among the signs and houses in his birth chart supports a smooth flow of energy related to this grand trine.

In contrast, astrological action loads the upper-left quadrant, the sector of public image and status, in Rudy Giuliani's birth chart. Much of this action originates in the 10th house, aspecting to the 11th, 12th, 1st, and 2nd houses. Rudy's *yang* Moon ☽ in Leo ♌ squares □ Venus ♀ in Taurus ♉, setting the stage for discord between work and home. And Mercury ☿ square □ Pluto ♀ suggests a resistance to the perspectives of others that results in disruptions and sometimes in adversarial relationships.

If you think you see a grand trine in Rudy's chart, too, you're right. There it is, linking his 10th, 2nd, and 5th houses. This is a lovely flow of energy supporting Rudy's ability to express himself professionally. But the imbalance of planets, signs, and corresponding energies makes it more difficult for this grand trine to express itself.

In or Out of Balance: 4, 6, and 10 Again

Squares □ and oppositions ♂ between planets of the 4th and 10th houses can signal a sense of imbalance in your life between work and home. Often the 6th house functions as the balancing point between conflicting areas of interest in career and home. You can see this in Jimmy Carter's birth chart. He has a number of challenging oppositions ♂ between his 4th and 10th houses. But he also has several sextiles ✳

from his 6th to his 4th houses, and one leg of his grand trine—a triple alignment of easy-flowing energy—linking his 6th and 10th houses. This helps to ease the tensions of those conjunctions and mitigate the challenges they present.

What Your Aspects Show About Your Houses of Career, Work, and Home

Although you can't change the aspects that appear in your birth chart, you can make choices about how you use the energy they represent. You can channel the turbulence of squares □ and oppositions ℰ for tremendous power and focus, just as we harness the power of rushing water to generate electricity. But you can drown in the still waters of trines △ and sextiles ✳, too. No matter what your chart shows, you still have to navigate!

So take a look now at the lines that might go across the center of your chart wheel between your 4th, 6th, and 10th houses. What aspects do you see? Write them here. You can practice your Astrology shorthand and write them using symbols: ♂ ✳ ♆; or you can just write out the words in the same formula format: Mars sextile Neptune.

Astro Houses	Planet	Astro Aspect	Planet	Supportive or Challenging?
_____	_____	_____	_____	_____
_____	_____	_____	_____	_____
_____	_____	_____	_____	_____
_____	_____	_____	_____	_____

Do you have mostly challenging or supportive aspects? Tally them here:

Number of supportive aspects: _____

Number of challenging aspects: _____

The Yin and Yang of the Tarot

Tarot cards can represent either *yin* or *yang* energy, depending on their context and the surrounding cards in a particular reading. Here are some ways you can begin to explore the *yin* and *yang* of the Tarot.

First, get your deck and separate the cards into Major Arcana (cards 0 through 21) and Minor Arcana (the four suits: Wands, Pentacles, Swords, and Cups). Let's start with the Major Arcana; set aside the Minor Arcana cards for now. Ready?

Yin and Yang of the Major Arcana

One way to look at the polarity of the Major Arcana cards is to have the card assume the polarity of its affiliated sign, *yin* or *yang*. A few of the cards are associated with more than one astrological sign, and so may contain within them both *yin* and *yang* influences.

Astrological Sign	Polarity	Tarot Major Arcana Card
Aries ♈	*Yang*	Fool, Magician, Emperor
Taurus ♉	*Yin*	Empress, Hierophant, Wheel of Fortune
Gemini ♊	*Yang*	Lovers
Cancer ♋	*Yin*	Temperance, Moon
Leo ♌	*Yang*	Strength, Wheel of Fortune, Sun
Virgo ♍	*Yin*	High Priestess, Hermit
Libra ♎	*Yang*	Empress, Justice
Scorpio ♏	*Yin*	Emperor, Wheel of Fortune, Death, Judgement
Sagittarius ♐	*Yang*	Chariot
Capricorn ♑	*Yin*	Devil, World
Aquarius ♒	*Yang*	Wheel of Fortune, Tower, Star
Pisces ♓	*Yin*	High Priestess, Hanged Man, Moon

One way to look at the yin *and* yang *of Tarot cards is to match them with their affiliated astrological signs, like yang Leo ♌ and Strength, and yin Capricorn ♑ and the World.*

Another way to look at the *yin* and *yang* of the Major Arcana is to let your Psychic Intuition assign the polarities based on what the cards represent to *you*. It's okay if these differ from the *yin* and *yang* of the cards' astrological associations. You might find, for example, that the Hierophant, astrologically *yin*, always has a connection for you with the quarterly financial reports you prepare—a job task that falls into the *yang* column. So for you, the energy of the Hierophant becomes *yang* in your Tarot readings. Over time, you'll develop an entire glossary of Tarot associations that are personal to you.

Take a few minutes now to see what associations come to mind for you as you explore the polarity of the Major Arcana cards. Start with the Fool, card 0. Hold the card in your hand as you look at it. Does it feel warm, bright, and action-oriented (*yang*) or cool, reflective, and intrinsic (*yin*)? Does the figure on the card seem feminine or masculine? Does the figure remind you of someone at work? Do you actually *feel* a sense of the card's energy? Write your perceptions in your Intuitive Arts Journal to start building your Psychic Intuition glossary for Tarot.

Yin and Yang of the Minor Arcana

Now let's do the Minor Arcana. Organize your deck's Minor Arcana cards by suit—Wands, Pentacles, Swords, and Cups. When you look at the suits, what sense do get about their *yin/yang* polarities? Wands and Swords are generally cards of action, giving them a *yang* influence collectively. Pentacles and Cups are more about receiving, giving these suits a *yin* influence.

The action-oriented suits of Wands and Swords are yang, *and the receptive suits of Pentacles and Cups are* yin.

Individual cards within any suit can be *yin* or *yang*, however, depending on how they appear in a reading. Take the Wands suit and hold the cards in your hands. Look at each card, one at a time. Does it feel *yin* or *yang?* Circle the *yin/yang* polarity you sense for each card in the following table. Remember, an individual card can have a different polarity from its Tarot suit.

Tarot Card	Wands	Swords	Pentacles	Cups
King	*Yin* or *Yang*	*Yin* or *Yang*	*Yin* or *Yang*	*Yin* or *Yang*
Queen	*Yin* or *Yang*	*Yin* or *Yang*	*Yin* or *Yang*	*Yin* or *Yang*
Knight	*Yin* or *Yang*	*Yin* or *Yang*	*Yin* or *Yang*	*Yin* or *Yang*
Page	*Yin* or *Yang*	*Yin* or *Yang*	*Yin* or *Yang*	*Yin* or *Yang*
10	*Yin* or *Yang*	*Yin* or *Yang*	*Yin* or *Yang*	*Yin* or *Yang*
9	*Yin* or *Yang*	*Yin* or *Yang*	*Yin* or *Yang*	*Yin* or *Yang*
8	*Yin* or *Yang*	*Yin* or *Yang*	*Yin* or *Yang*	*Yin* or *Yang*
7	*Yin* or *Yang*	*Yin* or *Yang*	*Yin* or *Yang*	*Yin* or *Yang*
6	*Yin* or *Yang*	*Yin* or *Yang*	*Yin* or *Yang*	*Yin* or *Yang*
5	*Yin* or *Yang*	*Yin* or *Yang*	*Yin* or *Yang*	*Yin* or *Yang*
4	*Yin* or *Yang*	*Yin* or *Yang*	*Yin* or *Yang*	*Yin* or *Yang*
3	*Yin* or *Yang*	*Yin* or *Yang*	*Yin* or *Yang*	*Yin* or *Yang*
2	*Yin* or *Yang*	*Yin* or *Yang*	*Yin* or *Yang*	*Yin* or *Yang*
Ace	*Yin* or *Yang*	*Yin* or *Yang*	*Yin* or *Yang*	*Yin* or *Yang*

Cards in the Balance

What do the cards have to say about the work/home, *yin/yang* balance in *your* life? Put all the cards in your deck back together. While shuffling them, ask the question: "Do I have balance in my work life and home life?" Shuffle the cards as long as you like. When you're ready, lay out the cards as you see here.

Record the cards and your perceptions and thoughts in the following table.

The first row represents your 4th house, the middle row represents your 6th house, and the third row represents your 10th house. What "story" do the cards for each house reveal? Do the cards remind you of people or events? Does each card feel *yin* or *yang?* Give yourself plenty of time to absorb the information the cards are giving you.

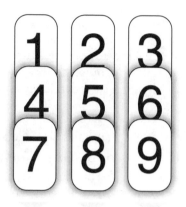

Your 4th, 6th, 10th House Balance Spread.

4th house   6th house   10th house
of home   of work   of career

4th House of Home	**Tarot Card**	**Yin/Yang**	**Perceptions**
Card 1	_____	_____	_____
Card 2	_____	_____	_____
Card 3	_____	_____	_____

6th House of Work	**Tarot Card**	**Yin/Yang**	**Perceptions**
Card 1	_____	_____	_____
Card 2	_____	_____	_____
Card 3	_____	_____	_____

10th House of Career	**Tarot Card**	**Yin/Yang**	**Perceptions**
Card 1	_____	_____	_____
Card 2	_____	_____	_____
Card 3	_____	_____	_____

Do the cards present a picture of balance or struggle? Do they represent how you feel about your work and its balance in your life? Do the cards reveal how your 6th house (your job) arbitrates balance between your 4th house (home) and your 10th house (career)?

chapter 3

True Effort Is Elemental

Elemental foundations
Every Element has a polarity, sign, house, and Tarot suit
A new perspective on Quality
Discover your astrological Workplace Elemental Essence
Psychic Intuition and Tarot reveal your co-workers' Elemental natures
Experiment with Elemental reactions—from going with the flow to
going up in smoke!

*The four Elements—Fire, Earth, Air, Water—are the foundation of
physical existence. They're also the foundation for how we get along
with each other (or don't) in the workplace. It's no accident that we
use the Elements to describe people, places, and events at work, both
positive and challenging, through terms like "an explosive exchange"
or "ideas that catch on like wildfire," a colleague at work who is
"fluid and flexible" or "air-headed," or an action plan that "grows
the business" or that "won't take root." You can use Astrology,
Tarot, and Psychic Intuition to see just which Elements are at work
for you—and how you can combine or separate Elemental influences
to make your job more fun and productive. (We have to throw that
in to make the boss happy.)*

Elemental Understanding

The four Elements—Fire, Earth, Air, and Water—give us what we
need to survive. Like the harmony of opposites we looked at in
Chapter 2 to achieve *yin* and *yang* balance in the way we approach
the push/pull of home and career, the Elements express their own

kind of balance within ourselves and in our work relationships. Elements themselves have *yin/yang* polarity. Fire and Air are *yang*—Fire is hot, bright, emboldening; Air is brisk, light, invigorating. Earth and Water are *yin*—Earth is dark, receptive, fertile; Water is soft, cool, soothing.

Of course, the workplace, like the rest of the universe, is not an environment of absolutes. Even when one Element dominates, the other Elements remain present. Understanding a co-worker's leading Element—and your own—gives you the ability to strengthen working relationships and find common ground when those relationships are challenging. Success—for work groups and companies as well as the people who bring them to life—requires blend and balance.

Here are some keywords that describe the Elemental workplace environment and the people you'll meet there.

Fire	Earth	Air	Water
Passionate	Grounded	Idealistic	Compassionate
Enthusiastic	Reasoned	Quixotic	Nurturing
Physical	Logical	Intellectual	Emotional
Creative	Methodical	Innovative	Intuitive
Forceful	Resistant	Objective	Immersed
Impulsive	Cautious	Detached	Passive
Bossy	Stubborn	Flighty	Moody
Forging	Rooted	Cloudy	Fluid

Now, let's look at each Element's associated polarity, signs, houses, and Tarot card suit.

Element	Sign	House	Polarity	Tarot Suit
Fire	Aries ♈	1st house of self	*Yang*	Wands
	Leo ♌	5th house of creativity		
	Sagittarius ♐	9th house of philosophy		
Earth	Taurus ♉	2nd house of values	*Yin*	Pentacles
	Virgo ♍	6th house of work		
	Capricorn ♑	10th house of career		

Element	Sign	House	Polarity	Tarot Suit
Air	Gemini ♊	3rd house of communication	*Yang*	Swords
	Libra ♎	7th house of partnerships		
	Aquarius ♒	11th house of humanitarianism		
Water	Cancer ♋	4th house of home	*Yin*	Cups
	Scorpio ♏	8th house of transformation		
	Pisces ♓	12th house of secrets		

Among co-workers, Elements that are alike—sensitive Waters, for example—tend to get along well with each other at first, as like attracts like. These co-worker relationships often are quite effective and functional—for a while. Without other Elements in the work group for counterbalance and inspiration, though, work quality can become routine or actually suffer. An intellectual, idealistic Air supervisor feels comfortable brainstorming with his or her Air employees, but may find the best team-building synergy comes from inviting into the discussion the solid planning of practical Earth employees, the flexible out-of-the-box intuitive hunches of Water employees, or the let's-take-action enthusiasm of Fire employees.

Tuning into the Elements will help you identify how the energies of Fire, Earth Air, and Water work in your workplace. If the Elements are out of balance in work groups, we often feel that we have to choose sides. The more polarized the personalities, the stronger the division of alliances may become. But harness the creative synergy of the Elements, and the sky is the limit!

Elemental Natures

Wands is the Tarot suit of work—the tools of one's trade. It belongs to the Element of Fire with an active *yang* nature and represents the astrological houses of self and creativity. Pentacles are representative of the fruits of one's labor and belong to the Element of Earth—the stable, receiving *yin* foundation upon which the astrological houses of work and career are constructed. Swords use *yang* energy to cut through to the heart of the matter; their Air Element takes flight in the astrological houses of communication and partnership. Cups flow their *yin* Water energy through the astrological houses of inner knowing and transformation.

Let's use the Tarot suits and your Psychic Intuition to tap into your Elemental impressions of your Elemental work self, your co-workers, and your company.

☯ Going through your Tarot deck so that you can see the images on the cards, pick a card that represents the essence of who you are at work at this very moment. Don't think about *why* you're choosing the card ... just go with what resonates for you, or feels right. And remember, it's the symbolic representation of the card's image, not the gender(s) of the people shown on the card that matters.

☯ Pick a card that represents your least favorite co-worker, the person who makes you turn and walk the other way when you see him or her coming down the hallway. Now, pick a card that represents your favorite co-worker, someone who brightens your day just by being at work.

☯ Pick a card that represents the company you work for and how that company represents itself to the world. Now, pick a card that best expresses what the environment of your department within the company or daily experience at work is like.

Record the names of the cards you've chosen, along with your perceptions, in the following spaces.

First card (you): _____

Element: _____

Perceptions: _____

Second card (least favorite co-worker): _____

Element: _____

Perceptions: _____

Third card (favorite co-worker): _____

Element: _____

Perceptions: _____

Fourth card (company): _____

Element: _____

Perceptions: _____

Fifth card (your work experiences in your department):

_____

Element: _____

Perceptions: _____

Take your time examining the cards, the Elements, and your perceptions of the imagery of each card and why you chose it. Are the Elements producing synergies among yourself, your company, your department, and your co-workers? Or is there friction that undermines Elemental power? Is it time for a promotion, a new job, or a move to a different department? What insights can you make into your workplace and how can you, or *should* you, apply your own Elemental energies to make your work more harmonious and in balance—for *you?*

Your Astrological Workplace Elemental Essence

You don't have to like your co-workers, but it's a good thing to at least get along for the eight hours a day that your jobs keep you together. Finding common ground—and it is there if you look deep enough (and we admit, sometimes you have to dig pretty far down)—is the first and most important step toward improving workplace quality. You can't change the people you work with, but you can change yourself and the ways that you interact with others in the workplace.

The Essence of Quality

Workplace jargon abounds with variations on the theme of quality, and now we're going to put yet another spin on the concept. In the Intuitive Arts, the Qualities join *yin/yang* and the Elements as a third dimension to understanding and explaining perceptions and motivations. There are three astrological Qualities: Cardinal, Fixed, and Mutable.

Quality	Signs	Houses
Cardinal	Aries ♈	1st house of self
	Cancer ♋	4th house of home
	Libra ♎	7th house of partnerships
	Capricorn ♑	10th house of career
Fixed	Taurus ♉	2nd house of values
	Leo ♌	5th house of creativity
	Scorpio ♏	8th house of transformation
	Aquarius ♒	11th house of humanitarianism
Mutable	Gemini ♊	3rd house of communication
	Virgo ♍	6th house of work
	Sagittarius ♐	9th house of philosophy
	Pisces ♓	12th house of secrets

Cardinal means prime. Cardinal folks are first out of the gate, the initiators, the idea people. They are ambitious, energetic, and determined—and if you can't keep up, they won't even notice they've left you behind! Although they see themselves as focused and invincible, the co-workers they leave standing in the dust might view them as, well, a bit self-centered and even egotistical. This is because those co-workers—inevitably reliable Fixeds and flexible Mutables—get stuck cleaning up their dust, putting details in order, and as often as not, finishing what their Cardinal colleagues start.

Fixed is steady, firm, unshakable. Your Fixed co-workers are the ones who leave staff meetings looking at their notes and nodding their heads. Were you watching out the window or doodling designs on your notepad when the boss handed out assignments? Fear not ... your benevolent Fixed co-worker will fill you in so you can do your part. As long as you do it the way your Fixed associate wants it done, that is. The other end of steady is stubborn, and it's the end you're likely to see when you circumvent convention. Not surprisingly, freestyle Cardinals and structured Fixeds often find themselves at odds.

Mutable means flexible. Mutables are the workplace peacekeepers, ever at the ready with resourceful solutions to head off conflicts or resolve problems. Their view is the big picture, and they excel in doing whatever it takes to make it manifest. It's hard not to like your Mutable co-workers; they are selfless and helpful, eager to give you whatever you need to get your work done. Of course, such generosity can be overwhelming; Mutables often find themselves with more to do than hours in the workday. This frustrates fast-moving Cardinals who can't bear to wait in line as well as methodical Fixeds who deplore inefficiency.

If you know the birth dates of the co-workers you identified in your Tarot Psychic Intuition exploration, you can add their Qualities (and your own!) to your notes. How does knowing the Qualities deepen your insights?

The Elements and Qualities of Colleagues

Partnership alliances come and go in the corporate world seemingly faster than marriages in the entertainment world. Find out your approach to workplace relationships by determining your astrological Workplace Elemental Essence. You need your birth chart, and, if you have access to the birth date, birth time, and birthplace of a work colleague, you can look at how compatible your Workplace Elemental Essences are!

We'll show you how by looking first at the astrological birth charts of two famous work partnerships to see what brings true partners together and what separated them.

When comedian Jerry Lewis and singer Dean Martin first took the stage together in 1946, it was a serendipitous pairing. Theirs seemed a match made in entertainment heaven. But it proved a turbulent partnership, and 10 years later it crashed to an end. The two did not speak to one another for more than 20 years. What set up their collision course with each other and fame, and what brought their partnership to an end?

Dean Martin's Birth Chart

Astro Planet In	Astro Sign	Element	Quality
Sun ☉	Gemini ♊	Air	Mutable
Moon ☽	Capricorn ♑	Earth	Cardinal
Ascendant	Pisces ♓	Water	Mutable

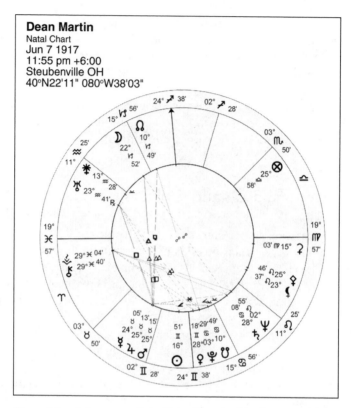

*Dean Martin's strong Sun ☉ in Gemini ♊, the Mutable
Air sign that guides communication, made him a natural
entertainer.*

With his natal Sun ☉ in Gemini ♊, the Mutable communicator, and
the Sun ☉ also ruling his 6th house of work, Dean Martin would *have*
to do something in the communication business. His Moon ☽ in Capricorn ♑, the Cardinal leader, his ascendant, or rising sign, in sensitive
and emotional Pisces ♓, the Mutable Water sign, tell us that this "something" would connect with others on a personal level. Writing, speaking,
singing, acting, making people laugh—the essentials of entertainment.
The Mutable Fire of Sagittarius ♐ on the cusp of his 10th house of
career (his midheaven) says that no matter what his career, Dean Martin
would make a strong showing and get people to become optimistic and
lighthearted about their lives. This same Sagittarius ♐ energy on Dean's
midheaven would want to educate, enlighten, and bring humor to the
public in any way possible. The majority of Dean's planets are within

the first six houses, so he would want to get people to look at the parts of themselves, of human nature, that relate to basic comforts.

Jerry Lewis's Birth Chart

Astro Planet In	Astro Sign	Element	Quality
Sun ☉	Pisces ♓	Water	Mutable
Moon ☽	Taurus ♉	Earth	Fixed
Ascendant	Cancer ♋	Water	Cardinal

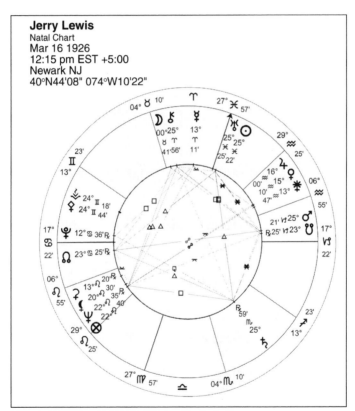

Jerry Lewis
Natal Chart
Mar 16 1926
12:15 pm EST +5:00
Newark NJ
40°N44'08" 074°W10'22"

The signs are all there for the grand master of laughter, Jerry Lewis.

Jerry Lewis's natal Sun ☉ is in Pisces ♓, the Mutable sensitive and happy Water sign. His Moon ☽ is in Fixed Taurus ♉, the organized and practical Earth sign. And his ascendant is in Cancer ♋, the Cardinal initiator and mothering or nurturing sign of Water. Family and people's lives make a huge impact on this comedian. He is easily moved and devoted to people who are emotionally or psychically down. He wants to make people laugh and cry and sing and dance. He has a need to be needed in society and his community. Cancer ♋ rising is a focus on family or extended family, so he wants to nurture his public image by doing humanistic work or work that uplifts others. With Sagittarius ♐ on Jerry's 6th house of work, Jerry's work has to be part of his philosophy of life. He has to *believe* in what he is doing is good for the greater group.

In the two charts, Sagittarius ♐ bridges Jerry's 6th house of work and Dean's 10th house of career, so both houses in each chart feed the other's career. And midheaven of Jerry's chart is Pisces ♓, Dean's rising sign! Both of their charts have Water rising signs, Cancer ♋ for Jerry and Pisces ♓ for Dean. When we saw these two together on stage or in public, we felt like they belonged together. We could feel their commitment to their work. They brought their own, and consequently our, emotions to the surface, and they sensed this in us and we in them. We saw them as equal partners who could change roles of dominance without confusing us.

So what happened with this dynamic duo? Here's how the Elements and Qualities in their birth charts match up.

	Dean Martin	Jerry Lewis
Sun ☉	Mutable	Mutable
	Air	Water
Moon ☽	Cardinal	Fixed
	Earth	Earth
Ascendant	Mutable	Cardinal
	Water	Water

Dean's Sun ☉ sign is in Air, signaling a need for private time and freedom. Jerry's needs are Water and Earth influenced, which are very different. Dean's flightiness and sometimes detached persona no doubt created problems for the two. If they had kept their relationship strictly business, it could have worked easier and possibly longer. But personal life came into play, and their differing values and lifestyles got in the way. What worked on the stage—ad-libbing and improvisation—just couldn't, and didn't, work out in real life.

Now let's look at another famous work alliance. Bill Gates and Paul Allen met in prep school in the late 1960s. The computer would eventually bind them in one of history's most successful entrepreneurial adventures: Microsoft. Although the two parted ways as business partners in 1983, they remain close friends.

Bill Gates's Birth Chart

Astro Planet In	Astro Sign	Element	Quality
Sun ☉	Scorpio ♏	Water	Fixed
Moon ☽	Aries ♈	Fire	Cardinal
Ascendant	Cancer ♋	Water	Cardinal

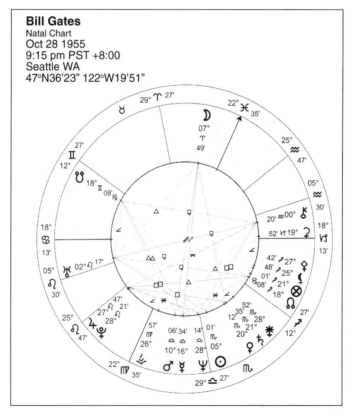

Bill Gates
Natal Chart
Oct 28 1955
9:15 pm PST +8:00
Seattle WA
47°N36'23" 122°W19'51"

The planetary alignments marking the birth of Bill Gates practically scream "entrepreneur!"

This is the chart of an innovative visionary who can lead and instill leadership in others. With his natal Sun ☉ in Fixed Water Scorpio ♏, we can see that Bill Gates is organized, focused, and intense about his work, his life, and his beliefs about what he can bring to the world. His fiery Cardinal Aries ♈ Moon ☽ tells us he is strongly self-motivated, ambitious, and independent. Bill lives and breathes his work, his contributions to society, and his focus to create. He is and always will be the workaholic, entrepreneurial figure we see today. But Bill has a softer side, too, thanks to his Cancer ♋ ascendant, an emotional Water sign that connects him deeply to family, immediate and extended.

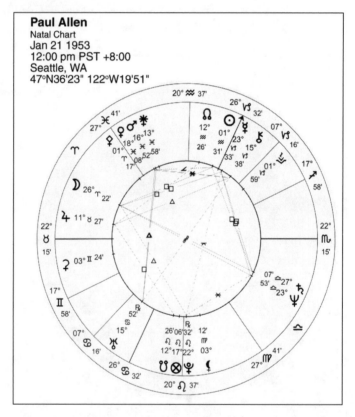

Although we might think of Paul Allen as the quiet partner, his noon birth chart shows that his mind never rests and he has an intense need to keep busy.

Paul Allen's Birth Chart

Astro Planet In	Astro Sign	Element	Quality
Sun ☉	Aquarius ♒	Air	Fixed
Moon ☽	Aries ♈	Fire	Cardinal
Ascendant	Taurus ♉	Earth	Fixed

Paul's natal Sun ☉ is in free-spirited Aquarius ♒, a Fixed Air sign that blends the eccentric with the cerebral. Paul is a creative and visionary thinker. It was Paul who came to Bill with that fateful issue of *Popular Mechanics* magazine advertising a build-it-yourself computer! Like Bill, Paul has his Moon ☽ in independent Cardinal Aries ♈, making work his life's focus. But with the Air and Fire combination in his personality (the persona of his ascendant and the inner self of his Moon ☽), Paul will want to venture onto many different paths in life—and has post-Microsoft. Aquarius ♒ has that eclectic, forget-the-rules orientation that needs constant stimulation.

Paul's birth time was not available, so Arlene cast a noon birth chart for him. The astrological information most likely to be inaccurate in a noon birth chart is the ascendant, as the rising sun that determines the ascendant moves into a new sign every two hours. Because of this, we did not include the ascendant in our discussion of Paul's birth chart or when we compared the charts of Paul and Bill.

Here's how the birth charts of Bill Gates and Paul Allen, certainly one of the twentieth century's most influential pairings, match up.

	Bill Gates	Paul Allen
Sun ☉	Fixed	Fixed
	Water	Air
Moon ☽	Cardinal	Cardinal
	Fire	Fire
Ascendant	Cardinal	Fixed
	Water	Earth

Look at the perfect match on the Moons ☽ for these two! Their inner selves are clearly simpatico, with Cardinal determination to blaze new trails and Fire to ignite ambition. And talk about spontaneous combustion—between Bill's Fire Aries ♈ Moon ☽ and Paul's Air Aquarius ♒ Sun ☉, we can see this pairing could accomplish great things. Water and Earth mix in their ascendants—fertile growth to support their shared creativity, originality, and vision. We can probably look for further collaborations between these two in the future.

Exploring Your Workplace Elemental Essence

Now, what's your Workplace Elemental Essence? You can do the same kind of analysis of your birth chart that we did for Dean, Jerry, Bill, and Paul. Once you have explored your own drives, passions, and work style, you are that much closer to realizing success in your work. Does your essential work nature match your own intuitive sense of your approach to work?

Your Birth Chart

Astro Planet In	Astro Sign	Element	Quality
Sun ☉	_____	_____	_____
Moon ☽	_____	_____	_____
Ascendant	_____	_____	_____

If you have a close work associate or partner who is willing to share birth information with you, you can go deeper still by looking at the relationships between your Elemental Workplace Essences that will advance or challenge your success together. You can compare your birth chart Elements and Qualities just as we did Dean's with Jerry's and Bill's with Paul's. You'll find out whether prospects are good for a long-term alliance, whether this is a one-shot union of short-term brilliance, or whether you'd be better off with a more compatible business partner!

The Tarot's Elemental Workplace Reactions

Now let's use the Tarot to look at how the various Elemental reactions produce beneficial, or dangerous, alchemy in the workplace. Do any of these pairings bring to mind people you work with now, or worked with in previous jobs? Where do you see yourself and your co-workers in these pairings?

Fire and Fire

Wands are the suit of Fire. The modern representation as a sturdy pole with a few leaves sprouting near the top belies the image's origin as a staff or torch—a green branch cleaved fresh from a tree so the staff itself would not burn, its end dipped in pitch to hold a flame to light the ancient nights. The sprouting leaves symbolize growth and renewal—the function of fire in nature, when it burns off overgrown fields and forests so new growth can flourish. The wand also represents the essence of an eternal flame. But Fire rules the 1st house of self with its competitive Cardinal energy, which can set up a clash of egos.

Fire and Fire: The King of Wands and the Knight of Wands can fuel each other in crisis but can ignite competitiveness and even hostility when there is no constructive outlet for their fiery energy.

In these two Fire cards, the King of Wands sits on his throne, wand in hand, looking out over his kingdom. He is a strong and capable leader, quick and decisive in his actions. His red hair symbolizes his fiery temperament. His wand almost looks like a torch, resting on the ground between his feet. The Knight of Wands grips his wand in one hand and the reins of his powerful horse in the other. Is he holding his horse back or spurring it on? In either case he is no doubt ahead of his group, either waiting impatiently for them to catch up or exuberant to be on the leading edge … alone.

Fire and Fire can be good for the short term in jobs that require rapid response to crises, such as firefighting or police work. But once the crisis is past, have the sand buckets ready. When Fire meets Fire, sparks fly. Although they may have strong respect for one another, a Fire boss and a Fire employee will butt heads at every turn of the way, with the Fire employee wanting to "take charge" and the Fire boss unwilling to relinquish any power.

Though quick to flare toward each other, Fire and Fire usually cool down when separated and can come back together relatively unscathed. Left to burn at each other, however, they can burn themselves out competing for resources. The astute boss, when two employees feature this Elemental combination, knows to cultivate creativity by letting these two flaming talents have relatively free rein to follow their inspirations.

Fire and Water

Cups are the suit of Water. Cups are caring, compassionate, and calming. They tend to go with the flow, as concerned about how co-workers or subordinates feel as about the work they're doing. Fire and Water are opposites, and opposites attract. Fire and Water pairings in the workplace are often efficient and productive, as each person brings a distinctive set of skills and abilities to the job. Ruler of the 1st house of self, Fire is all about ambition. Ruler of the 4th house of home, Water cherishes security and well-being. But the 1st and 4th houses share Cardinal energy, creating a bit of common ground between Fire and Water's natural opposition.

Fire and Water, the Queen of Wands and the Queen of Cups can be the perfect workplace complement as long as they maintain respect for their opposing approaches.

When we look at these cards, we see the Queen of Wands staking her claim, as it were, triumphantly displaying the fruit of her effort— a *sun*flower in full blossom, a symbol of Fire's role in growth and fruition. And this is no namby-pamby miniature sunflower, either, but a bloom as big as her own head! In contrast, the Queen of Cups sits at the water's edge contemplating the cup she holds in her hands. What does the cup contain? Dreams and ideas, no doubt! The Queen of Cups knows that careful nurturing has made possible the blooming sunflower the Queen of Wands holds, even as the Queen of Wands appears oblivious to all but the final product. The Queen of Cups, too, is pleased. She is comfortable and relaxed, content in the knowledge that she brings out the best in others.

Product and process—that's Fire and Water in the workplace. Hard-driving Fire, like the confident Queen of Wands, forges forward in pursuit of a goal. Never mind the challenges that might block the path … they just make the game all the more competitive, just what Fire loves. Contemplative Water knows that what lies beneath the surface can make all the difference, and follows intuition around obstacles.

Fire and Water make steam, which can be a steady source of energy to fuel work group or department activities. When the players fail to understand their opposing approaches to the work, however, this combination can fizzle into ineffectiveness. Each must respect and honor the other to maintain balance and productivity. Fire needs to remember that, as the cliché goes, still waters run deep … and that the Water appears still doesn't mean it is stagnant. Water, with its intuitive nature, might understand Fire's passion but find it too forceful. Out of balance, Water can extinguish Fire's creativity and enthusiasm or Fire can evaporate Water's visionary insights.

Fire and Air

Talk about spontaneous combustion! Swords are the suit of Air—it is Air, after all, that can cut through anything. Air can be soft and breezy or harsh and slicing. Airs are the idea people, always thinking of new ways to do things. And for the Air, there is always a new, a better, way! Fire's endless energy in tandem with Air's infinite innovations—this is a powerful workplace pairing indeed.

The Ace of Wands and the Ace of Swords complement each other's energies, reaching out from opposite sides of the heavens. Back to back, as here, or face to face, they present a balanced and formidable force.

Each Ace extends a hand from opposite sides of the heavens, the Ace of Wands from the right and the Ace of Swords from the left. Placed as we have them here, they are back to back in battleground formation. They cover each other front and back, creating between them a formidable whole. Switch their positions and they face each other. Are they acknowledging each other's power or at the ready to do battle? With this well-matched pair, probably both!

Fire and Air in the workplace are almost always effective combinations regardless of the hierarchy of their relationship—co-workers, boss-employee—because they so clearly feed each other. The Air employee supplies the innovative ideas that the Fire boss can make happen. Conversely, the Fire employee takes the Air boss's ideas and runs with them. This pairing becomes a problem only when other factors create challenges that their Elemental compatibility alone cannot overcome.

Opposing Qualities can show up in this pairing. Fire rules the 1st house of self and the 5th house of creativity, which are generally favorable alignments with Air's 3rd house of communication and 7th house of partnerships. Even though Fire rules both the 1st and 5th houses, these houses have different Qualities. The 1st house is Cardinal, while the 5th house is Fixed. Challenging tensions could arise between our Ace of Wands and Ace of Swords when work relates to matters that cross between the Cardinal energy of the 1st house and the Fixed energy of the 5th house—as might happen if the work is physical or creative, turning them to confront each other instead of working smoothly in collaboration.

Fire and Earth

Pentacles are the suit of Earth, representing the abundance that arises from hard work and careful cultivation. Earth rules both the 6th house of work and the 10th house of career, highlighting a focus on foundation. Earth also rules the 2nd house of values, representing the rewards of work—and telling us that those rewards come *from* work and effort. The *yang* of Fire and the *yin* of Earth establish these two Elements as opposites. And while opposites do attract, these two are not direct opposites in the same way as are Fire and Water—their attraction is more oblique. When focused toward a common goal, Fire and Earth can complement each other's efforts. Without such focus Fire can scorch Earth, searing it barren. Or Earth can smother Fire, suffocating its zeal.

The 2 of Wands relishes the abundance his efforts have created and looks ahead to new adventures, while the 7 of Pentacles admires the product of his nurturing labor and concentrates on the work still in front of him.

Red hat atop his head like flame on a match, the 2 of Wands looks out over the world he holds in his right hand to the world that surrounds him. With one staff in his left hand and the other anchored firmly to the wall of his castle, which seems to rise high above the other castles in his bucolic neighborhood, he has already built a degree of success and now waits to see the results of his actions. A tile mosaic of white lilies and red roses adorns the other side of the wall—a classic representation of the balance between *yin* (lily) and *yang* (rose), and between integrity (white) and courage (red). Is the 2 of Wands looking out over the sea, watching for an incoming ship? Or toward the distant mountains, seeking his next adventure?

Earthy 7 of Pentacles takes a moment to rest and enjoy the fruits of his diligent labor. Clearly he has tended his garden with care, keeping it clear of weeds and giving it the support it needs for growing tall and wide its crop of symbolic wealth. Notice how thick and substantial this vinelike plant is, with lush, broad leaves to soak up the sun and the rain that nourish its growth. The 7 of Pentacles is not finished with his work, of course; there is more planting to be done directly at his feet and perhaps in the field that stretches behind him. He's not looking either ahead or behind, however—he's focused in the here-and-now and on the tasks at hand.

In the workplace, Fire and Earth need but often don't appreciate each other. Fire's impulsive leap to action needs Earth's methodical planning to remain grounded in efforts that produce results. Earth needs Fire's enthusiasm to elevate caution to productivity. Fire and Earth must make the effort to see each other's strengths so each can support the other. When they can't do this, neither ends up being very effective. Fire becomes overwhelming and bossy; Earth stubbornly digs in.

Water and Water

Intuitive and nurturing, Waters create a work environment that is supportive and caring, ideal in jobs that require lots of human interaction. They are effective communicators, and their natural empathy encourages others to open up to them. Water rules the 4th house of home and the 12th house of secrets. Waters like to feel comfortable and secure, and for as intuitive as they are in sensing the needs and desires of others, they seldom share their own. When paired in the workplace, Waters generally work hard and efficiently, willing to do what it takes to get the job done.

Water and Water: The Knight of Cups and the Page of Cups go where the flow takes them.

The Knight of Cups is comfortable and poised on his high-stepping steed. He extends the cup he bears with the confidence of one who knows its contents are just what's needed. He is noble and compassionate, even a touch romantic in his view of the world. Wings on his helmet and his heels suggest perhaps more than occasional flights of fancy. The happy-go-lucky Page of Cups seems to not know what to do with the fish that's in his cup. Did he catch it or did it fortuitously land in his cup? Should he keep it or return it to the ocean behind him? Lacking structure to guide his decision, the Page of Cups is pensive and brooding—Water at its most challenging.

Water takes on the shape of its container. Without a container (structure!), water spreads out over whatever surface is there. As co-workers or in supervisor-subordinate relationships in loosely defined jobs, Water and Water combinations can pour forth effort that lacks results or become immersed in their thoughts and, like the Page of Cups, unable to move to action.

Water and Air

Have you ever seen a waterspout? This tornado over water is an impressive sight, with the swirling wind lifting the water right into the sky. But for the most part it's all about appearances, and soon enough the waterspout dissipates without consequence. So it can be when Water and Air partner. It takes just the right atmospheric conditions to blend these two together, and for a short time the show is spectacular. Both sets of our famous partners, entertainers Dean Martin (Gemini ♊—Air) and Jerry Lewis (Pisces ♓—Water), and techno-preneurs Bill Gates (Scorpio ♏—Water) and Paul Allen (Aquarius ♒—Air), are Water/Air pairings.

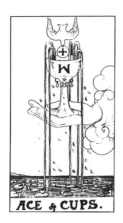 

The Ace of Cups and the Knight of Swords—Water and Air—can come together like a waterspout under the right conditions.

With Water ruling the 8th house of transformation and Air the 7th house of partnerships, a Water and Air fusion can pull its work group into extraordinary performances to rise to the need of special circumstances—a grand opening, for example, or a certification inspection. When the show's over, Water and Air return to their respective individual talents and abilities—which, although not so flashy, are considerable.

Filled symbolically from the heavens above, the Ace of Cups spills over into the lake below. Lily pads float on the surface, subtle evidence of the abundance that thrives beneath the surface as well—which, of course, is where the depth of Water's character resides anyway. The Ace of Cups renews and restores with great generosity. In storms the Knight of Swords, charging to action. When the two meet, we can imagine the Knight agitating the Cup's gentle flow into a vortex of activity. Water's intuition rises from the depths beneath the surface to swirl above, intensifying Air's brilliant, cutting-edge ideas.

The 1st and 7th houses that Water and Air rule, respectively, are Cardinal. These Elements won't stay melded for long; each has too strong of a pull to return to its own leadership. Water and Air co-workers get along fine when they can follow their respective strengths and approaches; with one deep beneath the surface and the other high above it, they can usually generate results that meet somewhere in the middle—close enough to grounded to be effective and productive.

Water and Earth

Water gives Earth its ability to produce results. It nourishes fertile ground, allowing Earth to become the womb that shelters and sustains the growing seeds of creativity. Water and Earth are both *yin*, embodying the essence of the maternal. Water rules the 4th house of home while Earth rules the 2nd house of values, establishing a structure of balance between work and home.

Water gives Earth its fertility. The generosity of the 2 of Cups makes possible the prosperity of the 9 of Pentacles.

The 2 of Cups represents the sharing nature of Water, the lifeblood of existence. This image is entirely symmetrical; draw a vertical line down its center, and each half contains complementary Elements. The exception is the house in the distant background, indicating that all of this sharing is for a common goal. The 9 of Pentacles represents the bounty of this sharing. The riches of material goods surround this elegantly robed woman, from the abundant grapes to the crop of gold coins. The tiny snail in the foreground subtly reminds that such prosperity arises from attention to detail and planned progress—the intrinsic domain of the Earth Element.

Too much Water, of course, creates ruin, turning the Earth to useless mud. Were the generosity of the 2 of Cups to overflow into the garden of the 9 of Pentacles, it would flood away all that careful cultivation (along with the hapless snail, who surely could not move fast enough to escape). Mud also immobilizes, slowing progress to less than a snail's pace. In the workplace, the emotion of Water can engulf Earth's logic and reason, causing Earth to bury itself in stubbornness and caution. This is where Water's intuition can identify when Earth has had too much, and hold back until Earth is ready to absorb more.

Air and Air

This match made in the heavens thrives on partnership. Air rules the 7th house of partnership, and its Cardinal Quality means that these co-workers are innovative and energetic. This is a great duo for making presentations or delivering training—these folks like to talk, and excel at getting their points across. What Airs tend to lack, however, is focus—and that can make them a challenging combination in the workplace. Without focus, the Don Quixote imagery of these cards easily becomes reality, with these two as likely to spend their time jostling windmills as engaged in productive activity.

The King of Swords and the Page of Swords, a classic pair of Airs, have the potential for great partnership although they bring to mind the gallant but out-of-touch Don Quixote.

Although the King of Swords holds his sword at the ready, he looks lost in thought. He gazes outward, but his eyes lack focus. His throne is high above the earth and even above the clouds, a band of which floats at the level of his head. The Page of Swords appears distracted and detached from his surroundings as well. The wind blows his hair back from his head and the tail of his tunic askew. Yet he stands with just one foot on the ground and his head in the clouds, staring off into the distance.

Air and Air typically get along fine in the workplace, often enjoying lengthy dialogues about technical details or esoteric concepts. How productive is all of this brainstorming? Well, that takes us back to the issue of focus ...

Air and Earth

This *yin* and *yang* pairing can bring an effective balance to the work group. Air and Earth can work together in ways that complement one another as long as they keep perspective on the other's viewpoint. Air brings ideas and concepts; Earth puts them to a reality check.

The Queen of Swords sits in regal glory on her throne, hand open to the wind that she rules, aloof and above the abundance of the earth beneath her. The clouds in the cold blue sky overwhelm the distant trees and a bird soars high overhead, perhaps bringing or sending messages. The Queen of Swords looks out over a vista visible to no one else, her sword at the ready to protect what she sees or maybe a warning that a sharp wind can cut to the quick before you even know what happened.

The Queen of Swords and the Queen of Pentacles, like Air and Earth, have less in common than many Elemental pairings.

By contrast, the Queen of Pentacles sits in the center of her abundance, surrounded by all forms of life. She holds with great care and appreciation a token of this prosperity, a disproportionately large golden coin. An arbor of flowering vines arches above her head, enclosing her into her landscape. Her feet rest firmly on the ground, unlike the feet of the Queen of Swords, which dangle in the air.

This can be another challenging combination in the workplace, however, as often it doesn't take long for this to become more than either can bear. Earth refuses to "do the work" of digging through Air's ideas to find the seeds of those that could be productive. Air feels rebuffed and suffocated, and turns aloof and arrogant. These two work together most effectively when they can respect each other's different approaches, which takes effort from each of them.

Earth and Earth

The Earth Element is hardworking and practical. In some respects, it's hard to have too many Earths in a work group or company. Earths are focused, reliable, and productive, not inclined to take many risks. They prefer the tried and true. As like attracts like, Earths typically get along well with one another and have great respect for each other's work habits and work ethic. The flip side of this is that Earths can have such an intense focus on the current goal that they can't see beyond it—or even to the sides of it. And if you're not quick enough to jump out of the way, Earth's determination will roll right over you!

Nothing says "hard work" like the 8 of Pentacles and the 3 of Pentacles.

The man on the 8 of Pentacles card is hard at work chiseling out another coin to join the ones already completed. He is intently focused on his work, with the coin he's working on propped on a wooden block for just the right angle as he taps the chisel with his hammer. An unfinished coin waits at his side. He wears a thick carpenter's apron to hold his tools and to protect his clothing from the flying chips. There is little to distract him from his work. The castle in the distant background might be the home that his hard work supports. The sculptor on the 3 of Pentacles pauses to check his work against the blueprint. He wants to be certain he is implementing the right pattern. Although his work dwarfs him, there are no distractions to divert his attention. Both cards present hard work and diligent effort focused toward building solid foundations.

Two Earths make a good pairing in situations that require carrying out instructions. Don't put these two in charge of making decisions or coming up with new ideas, though. It's not their strong suit, and it's likely to send them retreating to caution.

Elemental Work

Whether it's enthusiastic Fire, productive Earth, inventive Air, or sensitive Water, an understanding of how the Elements behave and interact can add a whole new dimension to how you approach work and the workplace—and don't forget Qualities, too! Now that you've read this chapter and determined your Workplace Elemental Essence, you are ready to harness these primal energies for success.

chapter 4

Attracting Success in the Work You Want

When I grow up I want to be ...
Your Sun ☉: your essential lifework
Your Moon ☽: your inner lifework
Your ascendant: presentation time
Your descendant: the partnership you
Your midheaven: your path to realizing your lifework
A Tarot horoscope reading

The right work makes the best use of your natural talents and abilities. This is where you shine, the stuff that is quintessentially you, at your happiest, at your most productive. Your job should feed the flame of the passion you feel for the work you love. Does it? Sometimes what you think of as your goals are really someone else's idea of what you should be doing—your boss, your co-workers, and your subordinates all have perceptions of what your job should be. (Not to mention all those outside influences like family and friends ...) Do you know your strengths and gifts? Are you ready to use them to attract the work you want? You might be surprised what your astrological birth chart reveals about your lifework ... and how the Tarot can stimulate your Psychic Intuition to lead you on the path of job satisfaction and career success.

What Do You Want to Be When You Grow Up?

Think back to when you were 7 to 14 years old. What did you want to be when you grew up? Can your mother pull out photograph after photograph of you with an open book on your lap—and now, all grown up, you are an editor? Were you obsessed with model airplanes—you knew *everything* about each one? Or were you the family expert on dinosaurs? Did you love to cook with your grandmother, or read *National Geographic* and imagine learning languages and setting off on exotic adventures? Today, does *your* childhood passion inform your adult lifework?

Saturn ♄, the planet that wants to put your nose to the grindstone, makes you aware of its presence for the first time somewhere around ages 7 to 14, depending on its position at your birth. Astrologers mark this as the time most of us form our first, and most uninhibited, perceptions about how we envision our lifework path.

Find pictures of yourself between ages 7 and 14. Are there clues in the pictures to childhood dreams and passions that are still with you today, even if they lurk deep down and go unacknowledged by your adult self? Can you find pictures of you dressed up pretending to be something? Even a Halloween costume. Were you a cowboy, a ballerina, a baseball star, a superhero, a doctor, a nurse, a soldier … a clown? Study the pictures. How do you look? What do you remember about the circumstances the pictures capture? When you think about the kid in the photos and then about yourself now, what do you feel? Do you feel a strong connection to, or estrangement from, your first hopes and dreams for your future?

Now that you *are* grown up, are you what you wanted to be when you were a kid?

From all the pictures you've gathered, select the one that evokes in your adult self now the strongest feelings of fondness and nurturing. What quality, expression, or activity in this picture draws you to it? Are you living now in harmony with the energy of that young you? Or does the picture show something you've lost, and want to find again? Carry this picture with you and let your Psychic Intuition build a bridge that stretches from your earliest hopes and dreams to your current hopes and dreams—pointing you forward as well, toward manifesting your best future lifework.

The Moment of Your Birth Holds Your Future

All that you see in your astrological birth chart reveals the characteristics that shape your abilities, talents, and interests. When it comes to understanding your personality and natural tendencies and talents as they relate to work and career, astrologers look at your Sun ☉ sign, Moon ☽ sign, ascendant, descendant, and midheaven. Each of these represents a facet of your identity, and each reveals its particular insights into your interests, motivations, talents, and potential challenges. As we look at each of these positions in your birth chart, we'll also use the synergy of the Tarot and Psychic Intuition to deepen and inform the discoveries you make about your essential self and attracting the life-work you want.

Although you might associate "your" sign as being your Sun ☉ sign, you—all of us—have 12 signs of influence in your birth chart. *How* they influence you depends on *where* in your birth chart they reside. Each sign's characteristics influence its placement in your astrological birth chart. A Gemini ♊ midheaven might influence you to go about developing your career from a foundation of flexibility and partnership, while a Capricorn ♑ midheaven is likely to see you push relentlessly in pursuit of your goals.

This chart shows the key traits for each of the 12 signs of the Zodiac.

Sign	Element	Quality	Ruling Planet	Characteristic Energies
Aries ♈	Fire	Cardinal	Mars ♂	Leadership, initiative, bold, enthusiasm, competitive, independence, determination
Taurus ♉	Earth	Fixed	Venus ♀	Persistence, goal-oriented, comforts, reliable, harmony, stability, loyalty
Gemini ♊	Air	Mutable	Mercury ☿	Intellectual, objective, big picture, curious, sharing, team-oriented, social, communication
Cancer ♋	Water	Cardinal	Moon ☽	Nurturing, serene, kind, comfort, tenacious, protective, emotional
Leo ♌	Fire	Fixed	Sun ☉	Leadership, strong, fearless, dynamic, fun, creative, loyal, ambitious, protective

Sign	Element	Quality	Ruling Planet	Characteristic Energies
Virgo ♍	Earth	Mutable	Mercury ☿	Practical, detail-oriented, modest, fair, sacred, duty, dependable, accurate
Libra ♎	Air	Cardinal	Venus ♀	Team-oriented, balance, peaceable, patient, cooperative, communication, loyal, diplomatic
Scorpio ♏	Water	Fixed	Mars ♂ and Pluto ♀	Probing, resilient, determined, goal-oriented, emotional, passionate, competitive, motivated
Sagittarius ♐	Fire	Mutable	Jupiter ♃	Exploring, open-minded, enthusiastic, independent, physical, generous, curious
Capricorn ♑	Earth	Cardinal	Saturn ♄	Hard working, pragmatic, goal-oriented, efficient, organized, grounded, fair, determined
Aquarius ♒	Air	Fixed	Saturn ♄ and Uranus ♅	Humanitarian, intellectual, idealistic, artistic, inventive, selfless, social
Pisces ♓	Water	Mutable	Jupiter ♃ and Neptune ♆	Compassionate, creative, visionary, intuitive, altruistic, dedicated, artistic, emotional

Each sign of the Zodiac has a corresponding Major Arcana card in the Tarot. As you learned in Chapter 2, some signs have more than one associated card, just as some signs have more than one ruling planet. Where this is the case, we've selected one Major Arcana card to serve as representative for our purposes in this chapter.

Astro Sign	Major Arcana Card	Astro Sign	Major Arcana Card
Aries ♈	Emperor	Libra ♎	Justice
Taurus ♉	Hierophant	Scorpio ♏	Judgement
Gemini ♊	Lovers	Sagittarius ♐	Chariot
Cancer ♋	Temperance	Capricorn ♑	World
Leo ♌	Strength	Aquarius ♒	Star
Virgo ♍	Hermit	Pisces ♓	High Priestess

Okay, with this information in hand, we're ready to look at how the Sun ☉, Moon ☽, ascendant, descendant, and midheaven influence your choices about work and career—and, how you can use that knowledge to bring you to the work you want, whether it be raising children, landscape gardening, marine biology, or public service!

Sun ☉ Sign: Your Essential Lifework

The Sun ☉ sign is the one piece of astrological information most people know about themselves. Your Sun ☉ sign is the astrological sign the Sun is in at the moment of your birth. It represents the essence of who you are as well as your potential.

Sun ☉ in Libra ♎: Bruce Springsteen

Rock legend Bruce Springsteen drew his first breath at 10:50 P.M. on September 23, 1949, in Freehold, New Jersey, his Sun ☉ nudging into the first degree of Libra ♎. Fourteen years later the youngster who would become "The Boss" of rock 'n' roll plunked down $18 for his first guitar and set off on the path of his muse—or should we say, music! Airy, Cardinal Libra is a creative, artistic influence, and its appearance also as Bruce's Moon ☽ sign as well as its alignment in Neptune ♆ and Mercury ☿ clearly signals the intense focus of this influence in Bruce's life. No matter Bruce's chosen life's work, his birth chart shows it will be imaginative and visionary. We often see Libra loading the charts of creative people.

Bruce's Astro Sign	Planet	Element	Quality	Tarot Card
Sun ☉ in	Libra ♎	Air	Cardinal	Justice
Moon ☽ in	Libra ♎	Air	Cardinal	Justice

71

Bruce's

Astro Sign	Planet	Element	Quality	Tarot Card
Ascendant in	Gemini ♊	Air	Mutable	The Lovers
Descendant in	Sagittarius ♐	Fire	Mutable	Chariot
Midheaven in	Aquarius ♒	Air	Fixed	The Star

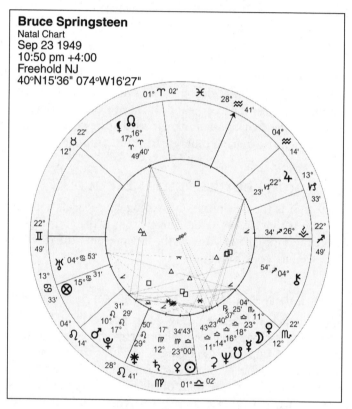

Bruce Springsteen
Natal Chart
Sep 23 1949
10:50 pm +4:00
Freehold NJ
40°N15'36" 074°W16'27"

With his Sun ☉ in Libra ♎ and 5 planets in Libra ♎ in his 5th house of creativity, Bruce Springsteen has the astrological support to be the talented and enduring musical artist he is.

Airy Aquarius ♒ at Bruce's midheaven gives him the ability to follow his dream's path wherever it takes him, from small clubs and smoky bars to the transformational stage of Madison Square Garden. But as talented as he is as an individual, Bruce's Sagittarius/descendant and his planets show us that collaboration is one of his strongest essentials, as his bond with the E Street Band attests.

72

His Gemini ♊ ascendant, under the rule of Mercury ☿ in Libra ♎, is a constant drive for Bruce to speak his mind about the human condition no matter what others might think, messages about life and work that reach us through songs like "Born in the USA" and "The Rising." His Sun sign's Major Arcana Tarot card, Justice, affirms Bruce's dedication to fairness and forthrightness even when the message isn't so popular. This is the chart of a born artist, a natural communicator, and an inquisitive mind.

Your Sun ☉ Sign

To identify your Sun sign, look for the ☉ symbol in your birth chart wheel, and the symbol for the sign in which it resides.

My **Sun** ☉ is: _____

Element: _____

Quality: _____

Ruling planet: _____

Characteristic energies: _____

_____

Tarot Major Arcana card: _____

Moon ☽ Sign: Your Inner Lifework

Your Moon ☽ sign reflects the inner you—your emotions and feelings. When your actions and reactions seem inconsistent with your Sun ☉ sign, it's often because you're responding from your heart and your intuition rather than from logic or reason. As the Moon cycles through the Zodiac every 29½ days, it spends just over 2 days in one sign before moving on to the next.

Moon ☽ energy is feminine, soft, flowing. Your Moon tells you a great deal about your approach in key areas of your life, particularly the one governed by the house where your Moon resides. Having your Moon in your 6th house of work, for example, might suggest that you'll be happiest in jobs that have to do with expression of emotion. Look for your Moon ☽ placement to gain insight into your deepest feelings and intuition about the lifework that fulfills your soul.

Moon ☽ in Libra ♎: Yo-Yo Ma

Famed classical cellist Yo-Yo Ma is well known for his collaborations with musicians as diverse as bluegrass instrumentalist Sam Bush and jazz vocalist extraordinaire Bobby McFarrin. His work with composer Tan Dun for the 2000 film *Crouching Tiger, Hidden Dragon* helped propel the movie's score to an Oscar and the soundtrack to a Grammy. So it should be no surprise to find Yo-Yo Ma's Moon ☽ in curious, sharing Gemini ♊. Ma's Sun ☉ (the planet of his essential self), Mercury ☿ (the planet that rules communication), Venus ♀ (the planet that rules beauty and art), and Neptune ♆ (the planet of inspiration and dissolving boundaries) are in Libra ♎. This artistic Libra ♎ lineup informed by a Gemini ♊ Moon ☽ tells us that this is the chart of a creative individual who has a deep inner desire to explore how he can share his talent with other artists, and with us.

Yo-Yo Ma's Astro Sign	Planet	Element	Quality	Tarot Card
Sun ☉ in	Libra ♎	Air	Cardinal	Justice
Moon ☽ in	**Gemini ♊**	**Air**	**Mutable**	**The Lovers**
Ascendant in	Sagittarius ♐	Fire	Mutable	The Chariot
Descendant in	Gemini ♊	Air	Mutable	The Lovers
Midheaven in	Libra ♎	Air	Cardinal	Justice

Yo-Yo Ma's expressive Moon ☽ in Gemini ♊ reveals the emotion of his artistic communications, with the delightful Lovers of the Tarot's Major Arcana overseeing his efforts. That this is a noon birth chart raises the slight possibility that Yo-Yo Ma's Moon ☽ sign is incorrect—the Moon ☽ moves at about 1 degree every 2 hours. Looking at the whole of his chart, however, Arlene feels this is an accurate Moon ☽ sign for this talented and emotional musician.

Libra's Cardinal energy supports leadership qualities throughout Yo-Yo Ma's natal chart, highlighting his ability to inspire others to follow *their* passions. Neptune ♆ rules music, and Yo-Yo Ma's Neptune in Libra ♎ adds more passion and spiritual focus to his work. Yet his Moon ☽ in Gemini ♊ allows him to *feel* with his head, not just with his heart, combining intellect and emotion in his creativity.

In Yo-Yo Ma's birth chart, notice all the planets that line up within 180 degrees, or half of the chart wheel; this shows a person who uses his gifts and talents with powerful intent. (Look back at Bruce Springsteen's birth chart and you'll see a similar "bowl" alignment.) Yo-Yo

Ma needs no outside motivation; his inner focus, his Gemini ♊ Moon ☽, urges him to create beauty and peace to share with the world, spoken in the language common to us all, music.

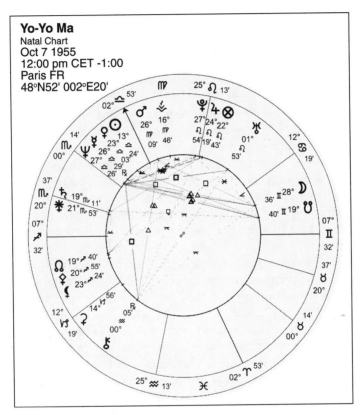

Cellist Yo-Yo Ma's Moon ☽ sign is Gemini ♊, although his chart shows significant Libra ♎ influences as well.

Your Moon ☽ Sign

To identify your Moon sign, look for the ☽ symbol in your chart wheel, and the symbol for the sign in which it resides.

My **Moon ☽** sign is: _____

Element: _____

Quality: _____

Ruling planet: _____

Characteristic energies: _____

_____

Tarot Major Arcana card: _____

Ascendant, or Rising Sign: Presentation Time

Your ascendant is the sign rising from the eastern horizon at the moment of your birth, beginning its climb into the heavens. It reflects the outgoing part of you, the part you make available to people who don't know you. Your ascendant reveals first impressions, what people think of you the first time they meet you. Your ascendant rules your 1st house of self, influencing your personality as well as your physical appearance. Knowing your ascendant will help you gain insight into what's important to you about how you present yourself in the workplace and in the world.

You must know your exact time and location of birth to pinpoint your ascendant accurately. This is because the Earth's rotation on its axis (not its revolution around the Sun), determines your ascendant. As the Earth completes 1 rotation every 24 hours, all 12 signs pass through the Zodiac each day—and the ascendant changes every 2 hours. If you were born as the Sun broke the horizon, your Sun ☉ sign and your ascendant are in the same sign. This intensifies the sign's influence over your essential self as well as your public presentation of who you are.

Your ascendant and your Sun ☉ sign can complement each other, or they can challenge one another. (Some might say "oppose," but we prefer to focus on the positive in such configurations.) For example, Cancer's ♋ Cardinal tenacity is the ideal match to bring out the Mutable compassion of a Pisces ♓ Sun ☉. A more challenging configuration might be Pisces ♓ rising with the Sun ☉ in Aquarius ♒, suggesting a need to direct conscious focus and effort toward interests and goals to avoid drifting from one job to another.

Capricorn ♑ Rising: Naomi Campbell

Supermodel Naomi Campbell was a typical teenager walking down the street when she caught the eye of a modeling agent. A few months later, her long-legged strides carried her down the fashion runway in Europe and, at age 18, onto the cover of *Vogue*. She's never looked back, with music CDs, movie and television roles, and even a couple books to her credit. Oh, and did we mention she co-owns (with fellow supermodels Elle Macpherson, Claudia Schiffer, and Christy Turlington) a chain of chic Fashion Cafés?

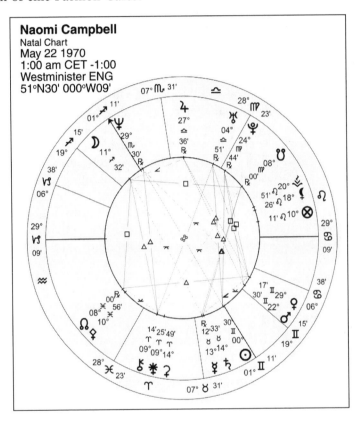

Naomi Campbell's Capricorn ♑ ascendant heralds determination, ambition, and earthy direction to guide this successful supermodel wherever she chooses to go.

Naomi's Astro Sign	Planet	Element	Quality	Tarot Card
Sun ☉ in	Gemini ♊	Air	Cardinal	The Lovers
Moon ☽ in	Sagittarius ♐	Fire	Mutable	The Chariot
Ascendant in	**Capricorn ♑**	**Earth**	**Cardinal**	**The World**
Descendant in	Cancer ♋	Water	Cardinal	Temperance
Midheaven in	Sagittarius ♐	Fire	Mutable	The Chariot

Naomi's ascendant is Cardinal Capricorn ♑, a persevering Earth sign that gives way to an enormously ambitious quality once she knows what she desires. This sign belongs to the Tarot's Major Arcana card the World, appropriately enough, as the world certainly belongs to Naomi. When this graceful, beautiful woman decides what she wants, don't stand in her way! She can climb over the biggest obstacles to success. Capricorn rising is known for directing the serious, thoughtful, and business side of life. Naomi's Gemini Sun trines her Capricorn ascendant ♊△♑, which gives even more drive and brings her strong communication to the forefront. Highly intelligent and skillful when it comes to being able to change her appearance or mood, she can certainly adapt or negotiate any roadblocks in her life or career.

Saturn ♄, her Capricorn ♑ ascendant's ruler, and her natal Sun ☉ in Gemini ♊ both fall in Naomi's 3rd house of communication in her birth chart—the house of media, travel, and promoting ideas. Naomi's very essence communicates beauty and is her best promotional tool. Fiery Sagittarius ♐ on Naomi's midheaven, combined with her emotional Moon ☽ in Sagittarius, gives some insights into that infamous temper. Her Moon's placement in her 10th house of career assures a certain amount of public notoriety. This is a woman we will notice throughout her career, no matter where her ascendant steers its path.

Your Ascendant

Your ascendant, or rising sign, appears on the outer ring of your chart wheel, on the cusp of the 1st house.

My **ascendant's** astrological sign is: _____

Element: _____

Quality: _____

Ruling planet: _____

Characteristic energies: _____

_____

Tarot Major Arcana card: _____

Descendant: Partnership at Work

Your descendant provides valuable insights about how and why you choose partnerships, vital information in work and career decisions. Your descendant is directly opposite your ascendant. It reflects the sign that was setting (descending) on the western horizon at the moment of your birth.

Your descendant's position on the cusp of the 7th house means your descendant rules your house of partnerships. It represents what you might consider important traits or traits you feel are lacking in yourself that you would try to accommodate by affiliating with others who do have them. It also reflects the tendency to surround yourself with people who are like you. In the workplace, these partners are co-workers, bosses, subordinates, and other professional colleagues.

A Presidential Descendant: George W. Bush

When George W. Bush was elected 43rd president of the United States in 2000, he became the second son in American history to follow his father's footsteps to the White House.

George W's Astro Sign	Planet	Element	Quality	Tarot Card
Sun ☉ in	Cancer ♋	Water	Cardinal	Temperance
Moon ☽ in	Libra ♎	Air	Cardinal	Justice
Ascendant in	Leo ♌	Fire	Fixed	Strength
Descendant in	**Aquarius ♒**	**Air**	**Fixed**	**The Star**
Midheaven in	Taurus ♉	Earth	Fixed	The Hierophant

George W's Sun ☉ in Cardinal Cancer ♋ gives him the drive to succeed and his fixed Leo ♌ ascendant the will to project his strength, while his Moon ☽ in Libra ♎ blends compassion with that drive. George W's descendant in Airy but Fixed Aquarius ♒ tells us that this president has strong opinions and tends to surround himself with those he considers comrades in arms or who are able to facilitate his goals. He is, like the Tarot card of his descendant, the Star. He wants people who are cerebral, futuristic, "think tank" people who share the common goals of his beliefs. A look at the Cabinet members he appointed after taking office shows an array of people who fit this bill. All are respected in their fields and each supports a facet of George W's political and philosophical agenda, even if their views differ among themselves—yet all are people he has known, even if not actually his friends, for a long time; many served in his father's Cabinet. George W's Fixed Taurus ♉ midheaven expresses the Hierophant's interest in social structures and morality.

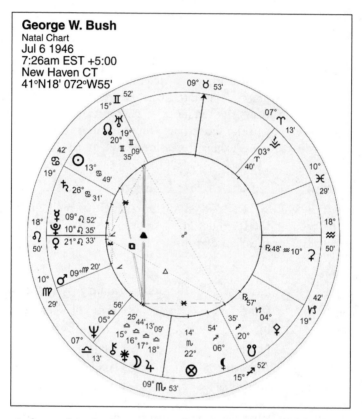

George W. Bush
Natal Chart
Jul 6 1946
7:26am EST +5:00
New Haven CT
41°N18' 072°W55'

A descendant in Aquarius ♒ shapes George W. Bush's desire to surround himself with people who share his ideals and goals, and yet can present him with information he can use to form the basis for his decisions.

Your Descendant

Your descendant is on the outer ring of your birth chart wheel, directly across the horizon from your ascendant, on the cusp of the 7th house (the line between 6 and 7).

My **descendant's** astrological sign is: _____

Element: _____

Quality: _____

Ruling planet: _____

Characteristic energies: _____

_____

Tarot Major Arcana card: _____

Midheaven: When I Grow Up I Want to Be ...

The astrological sign of your midheaven is on the cusp of your 10th house of career and rules this house, influencing the ways you approach your lifework goals and public recognition for your achievements. Whether you sort mail in an office or headline Hollywood hits, your reputation represents how well you connect the tasks of your job (your 6th house) with the path of your career (your 10th house). When this connection is strong, others see you as you see yourself. When you're working on this connection, there can be a considerable perception gap.

Paging Doctor, Er, Novelist Michael Crichton

Sometimes your route to your perfect lifework seems more convoluted than it is. Writer and producer Michael Crichton trained at Harvard to become a physician, writing his first novel *Andromeda Strain* while an intern there. Although he abandoned his medical career to pursue his calling as a writer (and later movie producer), Michael is firmly established as the master of the medical thriller—from the space-born infection that stars in his first novel to the genetic manipulations that return dinosaurs to modern times in the blockbuster *Jurassic Park*.

Michael's Astro Sign	Planet	Element	Quality	Tarot Card
Sun ☉ in	Scorpio ♏	Water	Fixed	Judgement
Moon ☽ in	Taurus ♉	Earth	Fixed	The Hierophant
Ascendant in	Leo ♌	Fire	Fixed	Strength
Descendant in	Aquarius ♒	Air	Fixed	The Star
Midheaven in	**Aries ♈**	**Fire**	**Cardinal**	**The Emperor**

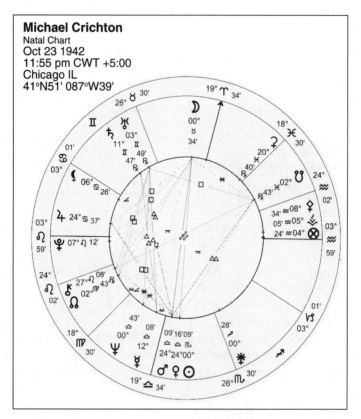

Author Michael Crichton's Aries ♈ midheaven leads him to chart his own course.

Michael's trailblazing Aries ♈ midheaven and his strong Leo ♌ ascendant lead the way into new storytelling genres. Michael's Sun ☉ in Scorpio ♏ in his 4th house of home, which governs psychological foundations, drives his ability to ferret out the secrets of science that most terrify us, and his intellectual Aquarius ♒ descendant seeks the full complement to his imaginings. The Emperor rules Michael's Aries ♈ midheaven, a perfect image for this writer who is a master at feathering out information about the human condition in ways that surprise and entertain us.

Your Midheaven

Your midheaven is on the outer ring of your chart wheel, on the cusp of the 10th house.

My **midheaven's** astrological sign is: _____

Element: _____

Quality: _____

Ruling planet: _____

Characteristic energies: _____

_____

Tarot Major Arcana card: _____

Using Astrology to Attract the Work You Want

From looking at the birth charts of rocker Bruce Springsteen, cellist Yo-Yo Ma, supermodel Naomi Campbell, 43rd U.S. president George W. Bush, and writer-producer Michael Crichton, you've gotten a pretty good idea of how their astrological influences reveal their essential natures and inform their path of lifework. Now it is time for you to look at how *your* Sun ☉, Moon ☽, ascendant, descendant, and midheaven influence *your* choices of work and career. Complete the following table.

Your Astro Sign	Planet	Element	Quality	Tarot Card
Sun ☉ in	_____	_____	_____	_____
Moon ☽ in	_____	_____	_____	_____
Ascendant in	_____	_____	_____	_____
Descendant in	_____	_____	_____	_____
Midheaven in	_____	_____	_____	_____

What do you see that supports or challenges your efforts to attract your essential lifework?

A Tarot Horoscope Reading

Tarot and Astrology, seen through Psychic Intuition's lens of inner knowing, reveal so much that helps you in understanding yourself and the choices you make about your job and career. Okay, though, so you've been able to identify what *kind* of work you want to attract, but ... will you make any money at it?

  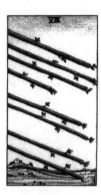

Tom's question: "Where is my career headed this year?"

Three-Card Tarot Prosperity Reading

For this reading, draw three cards from your Tarot deck, one card at a time. The first card represents your 2nd house of values and money, the second card represents your 6th house of work, and the third card represents your 10th house of career. We asked Tom to see what prosperity lay ahead in his work choices.

Card 1 representing the 2nd house of values and money: 4 of Cups R. This card says that Tom will come out of a contemplative state about his finances and values, starting a new direction this year; the 4 of Cups in a reversed position indicates a job or work assignment coming to an end. Tom will have new offers that bring in extra money.

Card 2 representing the 6th house of work: Ace of Pentacles. Tom is making headway to a new foundation; it is clear he desires new growth in his present workplace, or will expand his skills in a new workplace. He is at a new beginning for prosperity, wealth, or a business idea. If additional education or training is needed, the encouragement or financing to get it is on the way.

Card 3 representing the 10th house of career: 8 of Wands. Tom's career is about to take flight. This year he will accomplish his career goals, with approval and recognition from the outside world. This card encourages Tom to stay the course, as his present goals are about to become reality. Ask for help where you need it, this card tells Tom; it is there for you.

One Year to the Work You Want

At the beginning of this chapter, we showed you the wheel of the Zodiac and the Major Arcana cards that correspond to each of the 12 astrological signs. Now, you're going to do Tarot's Horoscope Spread, a tour through the 12 astrological houses, month by month, to see what is in store for your plan to attract the work you want in the coming year. As you shuffle the deck, meditate upon all you've learned in this chapter about yourself and your lifework path. When you are ready, deal the cards as shown, beginning with the 1st house and continuing counterclockwise until you've laid out a card for each house, or month of the year.

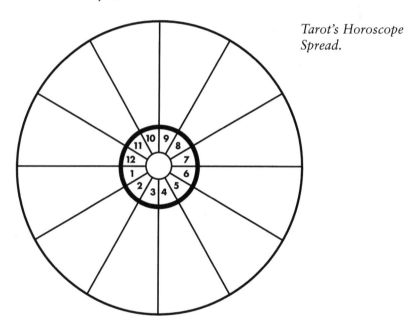

Tarot's Horoscope Spread.

First, look at each card, one at a time, in connection with its house placement. How does the imagery of the card and the message it conveys correspond to the area of life that house represents? How does this message support or challenge your work goals for the year?

1st house (self) card: _____

Message: _____

2nd house (values and money) card: _____

Message: _____

3rd house (communication) card: _____

Message: _____

4th house (home) card: _____

Message: _____

5th house (creativity) card: _____

Message: _____

6th house (work) card: _____

Message: _____

7th house (partnerships) card: _____

Message: _____

8th house (transformation) card: _____

Message: _____

9th house (beliefs) card: _____

Message: _____

10th house (career) card: _____

Message: _____

11th house (life goals) card: _____

Message: _____

12th house (secrets) card: _____

Message: _____

Second, look at the relationships between the houses. For example, looking at the Tarot card in the Horoscope Spread for your 2nd house of values in connection with the card you chose for your 6th house of work reflects not only the relationship between your earnings and your job, but also between your abilities—your personal assets—and how you apply them to your job.

☉ 2nd house of money and values Tarot card: _____

6th house of work Tarot card: _____

Pair Message: _____

☉ 2nd house of money and values Tarot card: _____

10th house of career Tarot card: _____

Pair Message: _____

☉ 6th house of work Tarot card: _____

7th house of partnership Tarot card: _____

Pair Message: _____

☉ 6th house of work Tarot card: _____

10th house of career Tarot card: _____

Pair Message: _____

☉ 7th house of partnership Tarot card: _____

10th house of career Tarot card: _____

Pair Message: _____

Now look at each card in the Horoscope Spread so that it corresponds to a month of the year, starting with 1 for January through 12 for December. Viewed this way, what monthly goals and priorities emerge for your year plan to attract the work you desire?

January's Tarot card: _____

Month's Goals and Priorities: _____

February's Tarot card: _____

Month's Goals and Priorities: _____

March's Tarot card: _____

Month's Goals and Priorities: _____

April's Tarot card: _____

Month's Goals and Priorities: _____

May's Tarot card: _____

Month's Goals and Priorities: _____

June's Tarot card: _____

Month's Goals and Priorities: _____

July's Tarot card: _____

Month's Goals and Priorities: _____

August's Tarot card: _____

Month's Goals and Priorities: _____

September's Tarot card: _____

Month's Goals and Priorities: _____

October's Tarot card: _____

Month's Goals and Priorities: _____

November's Tarot card: _____

Month's Goals and Priorities: _____

December's Tarot card: _____

Month's Goals and Priorities: _____

chapter 5

Do What You Love and the $$ ...

Rewrite your job description
Psychic Intuition and your perfect workday
Signs that support, signs that challenge
Synastry: Astrology explores your relationship to your work
Tarot reveals what's happening on the job
Are you compatible with your work?

The U.S. Department of Labor lists more than 820 occupations, and the numbers of different jobs available within each makes even a statistician's head spin. Your job might be a singular passion that shapes what you choose to do to earn a living—you'd do it anyway, even if you didn't get paid for it! Or you might be punching the clock, marking the hours until you are "released" to the real stuff of living, like caring for your home and family. Perhaps the job is merely a way to earn the money to pay for your true passions—travel, writing novels, building a deck on the house. In this chapter, we explore synastry, the branch of Astrology devoted to relationships, to see whether your current work supports or challenges your lifework. A Tarot reading will deepen your insights. We use Psychic Intuition to visualize your perfect workday. Whatever your job description, the Intuitive Arts can help you make the most of the work you do—and maybe even help transform the experience of work to have greater meaning and purpose for your life goals.

So What Do You Do?

Finding the *perfect* job is a process of matching your talents and interests with companies willing to pay for them. Or if takers are in short supply and you have the resources, building your own company—even if you're its only employee! Now, maybe your current job isn't *perfect,* but whose is? Some days it may seem like you and your colleagues are in the flow, ideas abound, and the excitement is exhilarating. Other days may seem interminable, nothing goes right, and even Dilbert (from the comic strip) has it better than you do! As in personal relationships, your relationship to your work has its ups and downs. But ... do you love (or even like) what you do? And ... exactly what *is* it that you do every day?

A Day in the Life of Your Perfect Job

Before beginning this Psychic Intuition exercise, we want you to focus on your job description. In the space provided, write a description of what you do, whatever that is—from being a student, to caregiving for an elderly parent, to raising kids, to running the show, to writing and filing those reports, to signing the checks. Your workday might include multiple jobs, such as bank teller by day, hospital volunteer a few evenings a week, and community garden duties on weekends.

List all your jobs and what you do—and we mean this literally. What do you *do* while you are working? Where do you go? Who are you with? What is the goal of your work? When you're done, read the descriptions and go back and add how you feel about what you do. Do you *enjoy* standing all day? Do you *enjoy* working in front of the computer? Do you *enjoy* flying all over the country to meetings and conferences? Do you *love* what you do? We've listed space to include as many as three jobs—that's enough work!

Job 1: _____

Feelings: _____

Job 2: _____

Feelings: _____

Job 3: _____

Feelings: _____

Do any of the jobs you've listed have a formal job description? If so, compare that description to the one(s) you wrote to see if you're in tune with your company's idea of what you should be doing at work. Have you used the same nouns and verbs your formal job description uses? Do you like your company's formal job description? Or is it something you try to work around (and how successful a strategy has that been for you)?

Now, get comfortable. For the next 10 minutes, you're going to use your Psychic Intuition to *live* your perfect workday on the job. We'll use guided visualization to accompany you through your day. If you can, audiotape the visualization text and play it to yourself while you meditate, fully immersing yourself in your most fulfilling work experience. If you're going it alone, read the visualization several times before you begin, so you can then indulge your vision without interruption.

Take three slow, deep, cleansing breaths.

> *See yourself getting out of bed, showering, dressing. What clothes are you wearing? It doesn't matter if they aren't yet in your wardrobe. For right now, they're hanging in your closet, waiting for you. Do you have coffee, eat breakfast? Smell the coffee ... taste the Krispy Kreme (or the fresh melon and strawberries or the oatmeal with brown sugar and raisins; it's the start of your perfect workday, so have what you like). Who is at home? Are you alone, with a partner or spouse, or fixing cereal for the kids? See your prework morning unfold in synchronous, beautifully timed and blissfully coordinated glory.*
>
> *Now, you are on the way to work. How do you get there? Do you walk, drive, or take the subway or bus? Does someone drop you off at work—or do you have to drop off a spouse or child on the way to your work? Is the commute a source of stress or is it something you look forward to every day? Imagine your journey to work unfolding optimally, as you arrive at the office on time, refreshed, and ready to start the workday.*
>
> *Where is your workplace? What colors are there? What smells? If outdoors, what's the season, the temperature, the foliage? If indoors, what's the decor, the layout? Do you have an office ... with a door? With a window? With corner windows? Someone comes to greet you. Who is it, what is his or her name? Why is this person there? Bringing you the day's agenda, work assignments, contracts to sign, fresh cup of coffee? Conjure details that allow you to use all of your senses as you experience your first 15 minutes at work.*
>
> *Let your vision take you through the entire day. Remember, this is your perfect day on the job, so let your mind envision the best potential your job holds to deliver that experience for you. Do you prefer structured break times, or can you break when you*

*desire? Is your day full of meetings, or do you spend much of
your time alone engrossed in what it is your responsibility to do?
Are you a supervisor? Or do you prefer to work for someone
else? What do you do for lunch? How is your afternoon different
from your morning, or is it more of the delightful same (whatever
that is)? Do you work more than one job or shift? When it's time
to call it a day, do you want to leave, or stay? How do you feel
as you leave the workplace? Do you go out with colleagues or
meet friends or your significant other? Or do you head home to
make dinner and help the kids with homework?*

*As you arrive safely home, you are welcomed and greeted
warmly. You feel energized and acknowledge a sense of accomplishment for a good day's work, well done.*

Can you see yourself living this perfect day? You might be surprised
at how fast the gap closes when you begin to explore the possibilities
for transforming vision into reality. Here's a homework assignment:
Find an item that you feel represents your perfect workday, something
that carries a positive energy every time you see it, touch it, or even
hear it—it could be a song. Carry this item in your pocket, briefcase,
purse ... put it on your desk ... hang it on your wall ... play the CD.
Consider this item a sacred symbol of your aspirations and your ability
to manifest your best workday as your reality.

Having your perfect experience of work always within reach of your
Psychic Intuition keeps you primed to notice and take advantage of
opportunities that present themselves—and this may be a new job,
if the one you have makes it impossible for you to imagine *anything*
perfect about it! Jupiter ♃, the planet of expansion, might bless you
with incredible luck that lets you leap into your perfect job, or, like
Tarot's Fool, keep walking your path toward it, one step at a time,
until you get there.

A Match Made in Heaven,
or Get Me Outta Here!

Here are some general work characteristics that the energies of each
astrological sign support or challenge. First, we want you to cover
the two left columns so you can't see them. Focus on the two right
columns. Read the descriptors, and put circle words or phrases wherever you find yourself saying, "Hey, that's my job!" Circle as many as
apply in each column.

When you're finished, uncover the left columns. How do the astrological signs, corresponding Tarot cards, and their energies either support or create challenges for *your* work situations? What associations can you make? Is your boss a Cardinal Aries ♈ Emperor who facilitates teamwork that fires up ideas, or who, as the Emperor reversed, imposes strict rules that have everyone worried about *getting* fired? Does your workplace environment feel more like a Cancer-inspired ♋ supportive family, patient and loving as Tarot's Temperance upright? Or is it expressing the energy of Tarot's moody Moon reversed?

Astro Sign and Tarot Card	Element/ Quality	Supports Work That Involves*	Challenges Work That Involves*
Aries ♈ *Fool, Magician, Emperor*	Fire Cardinal	Autonomy, initiative, project leadership, getting things started, multiple activities, adventure, risk, competition, physical activity	Strict procedures, single focus of effort, repetition, implementation, quiet environment, maintaining, status quo
Taurus ♉ *Empress, Hierophant, Wheel of Fortune*	Earth Fixed	Long-term focus and effort, seeing things through from start to finish, organization, structure, tangibility, continuity, predictability	Fragmented tasks or projects, inconsistent procedures or standards, theoretical concepts, chaotic environment
Gemini ♊ *Lovers*	Air Mutable	Strategic planning, group presentations, public speaking, investigation, research, collaboration	Solitude, isolated job tasks, repetition, lack of big picture context, confrontation
Cancer ♋ *Temperance, Moon*	Water Cardinal	Teaching or training, problem-solving, quiet environment, group interactions	Loud or harsh environment, discord, technical details, limited contact with other people
Leo ♌ *Strength, Wheel of Fortune, Sun*	Fire Fixed	Mid- and upper-level management, people leadership, activity, fun, initiative, dedication	Formal environment, anonymity, small circle of work associates, arbitrary constraints, micro-management

Astro Sign and Tarot Card	Element/Quality	Supports Work That Involves*	Challenges Work That Involves*
Virgo ♍ *High Priestess, Hermit*	Earth Mutable	Details, rules, precise procedures, repetition, organization, accuracy, tangibility, structure	Unstructured environment, inconsistency, disorder
Libra ♎ *Empress, Justice*	Air Cardinal	Team orientation, cooperation, patience, tact, fairness, analytical thinking, intellect	Conflict, isolation from other people, inequity, boisterous environment, snap decisions
Scorpio ♏ *Emperor, Wheel of Fortune, Death, Judgement*	Water Fixed	Goals and objectives, competition, self-motivation, endurance, targeted investigation or research	Repetition, collaboration, management-by-committee, ambiguity
Sagittarius ♐ *Chariot*	Fire Mutable	Getting along with people, travel, independence, flexibility, continual learning, big picture concepts	Isolation from other people, details, physical inactivity, repetition
Capricorn ♑ *Devil, World*	Earth Cardinal	Intense effort and focus, pragmatic decisions, goals and objectives, persistence, objectivity, efficiency	Unstructured environment, laxness, waste, lack of commitment
Aquarius ♒ *Wheel of Fortune, Tower, Star*	Air Fixed	Idealism, selflessness, getting along with and being around other people, inventiveness, "for the common good" orientation	Strict rules, egotism, status, hierarchy, "one right way" orientation
Pisces ♓ *High Priestess, Hanged Man, Moon*	Water Mutable	Visionary concepts, connectedness to other people, comfortable environment, occasional solitude	Clamor and confusion, details, mechanical devices, narrow focus of work effort, constant activity

Note: Upright Tarot cards represent support; reversed Tarot cards indicate challenge.

Synastry: How Is Your Relationship to Your Company?

Did you know that your company has a birth chart, too? It's calculated from the time of its initiation, typically the date, place, and time of its incorporation. By examining your birth chart and the chart for your company (or a company you'd *like* to work for), you can see where you mesh and where you clash ... and even catch a glimpse of your future together. Maybe you *are* the company, and synastry, Astrology's study of relationships, can reveal insight into how harmonious your entrepreneurial endeavor will be. A synastry grid compares astrological aspects (the relationships between planets) between two birth charts to reveal areas of support or challenge that emerge.

Exploring Aspects: The Synastry Grid

We talked about the five main astrological aspects—conjunction ☌, sextile ✶, square □, trine △, and opposition ☍—in Chapter 2. Here, we're adding a sixth, quincunx ⚻. Here's a summary of what the major aspects mean. Beneath each aspect, we've identified a Tarot card that represents the aspect's energy.

Major Astro Aspect	Degree of Separation	Keywords
Conjunction ☌ *Wheel of Fortune*	Within 10° of each other	Harmonious or challenging, depending on the planets
Sextile ✶ *7 of Pentacles*	60° from each other	Favorable in supporting your interests in what the planets represent
Square □ *Death*	90° from each other	Challenging, even harsh, but presents the greatest opportunities
Trine △ *Ace of Cups*	120° from each other	Propitious, allowing things to happen seemingly without effort
Quincunx ⚻ *Magician*	150° from each other	Challenging, with no connection between the planets, requires adjustments
Opposition ☍ *7 of Wands*	180° from each other	Confrontational, but presents opportunities if you can work through the challenges

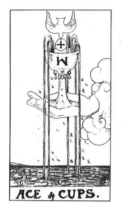

ACE of CUPS.

With a trine △, good things flow in seemingly endless abundance with respect to the aspected planets—like Tarot's Ace of Cups.

THE MAGICIAN.

What do you do with a quincunx ⊼? Only Tarot's Magician knows! Create the right environment for these unaligned planets to share energy.

Sextiles ✶ suggest you can get what you want if you put forth enough effort to spur their energy, like the farmer in the 7 of Pentacles.

Where there's an opposition ☍, there's likely to be a battle. Like Tarot's 7 of Wands, you can turn it into alliance.

WHEEL of FORTUNE.

Spin the Wheel of Fortune when a conjunction ☌ shows up. This aspect's energy can either support or thwart your efforts.

DEATH.

You must change, usually in a big way, to receive the opportunity Tarot's Death or a square ☐ brings—but it can be the opportunity of a lifetime.

To use synastry to find your compatibility ratio to your company or job, we're going to look at the personal planets and the outer planets.

Personal Planet	Astro Symbol	Key Influence
Sun	⊙	Identity
Moon	☽	Passion
Mercury	☿	Communication
Venus	♀	Money
Mars	♂	Personal power

Outer Planet	Astro Symbol	Key Influence
Jupiter	♃	Prosperity
Saturn	♄	Longevity
Uranus	♅	Originality
Neptune	♆	Vision
Pluto	♇	Transformation

To see how a person and a company get together through synastry, let's consider the supportive partnership between Bill Gates and Microsoft. We already explored Bill's relationship with partner Paul Allen in Chapter 3. Paul, of course, moved on to other ventures—as we might expect with his Aquarius Sun ♒ ⊙ and the entrepreneurial energy of his Aries Moon ♈ ☽. But what's kept the equally driven Bill (who, as you might recall, shares Paul's fiery Aries Moon) with Microsoft? Because the precise time of Microsoft's incorporation is unknown, Arlene cast a noon birth chart for Microsoft. It's very likely that the company's incorporation papers were filed within three or four hours of noon, during normal business hours, making the chart information fairly accurate.

The aspects among the personal planets show us the common bonds between the person and the company—in this case, between Bill Gates and Microsoft. The more aspects there are, the more intense and personal the attachment, giving the relationship an emotional focus or a passionate connection. When we're looking at a synastry grid for a person and the company that person created, as we are here, we'd expect to see the same kinds of connections among their personal planets as we might see between a parent and a child or between two personal partners. And good heavens, do we ever!

Across
Bill Gates
Natal Chart
Oct 28 1955
9:15 pm PST +8:00
Seattle WA
47°N36'23" 122°W19'51"

Down
Microsoft Inc.
Natal Chart
Jun 25 1981
11:59 am PDT +7:00
Redmond WA
47°N40'27" 122°W07'13"

	☽	☉	☿	♀	♂	♃	♄	♅	♆	♇	⚷	⚶	⚴	⚵	⚳	☊	☋	As	Mc	⊗	⚸
☽	☌ 4S12		☍ 4A34		☍ 1S54	⚼ 0A47		△ 9S43		⚼ 1A21				⚼ 1A52		△ 6A08		□ 6A13		△ 9A01	
☉	□ 3A42	△ 0A54		⚼ 1A05	□ 6A00		⚼ 2A29		△ 5S52				☍ 6S24								
☿		△ 6S32				⚹ 0A41			△ 0A14	⚹ 0A07	⚻ 1S52	□ 1A31	☍ 0A46	⚻ 0S24					□ 5A54	☍ 7A27	☍ 2A40
♀				△ 4S52			△ 3S28	☌ 7A14	□ 3A11		☍ 5A16	⚹ 1A53	⚻ 2A39	△ 3A48	☍ 5S12			☌ 6S50	△ 2S29		⚻ 0A45
♂			△ 2A04		△ 4S24			∠ 2A47	⚼ 1S16		⚼ 0A49					☍ 3A38	☌ 3A38			☍ 6A31	
♃	☍ 6A08				☌ 8A26			⚹ 0A37			△ 1S21	☌ 4S43	□ 3S58	⚹ 2S49							□ 5S52
♄	☍ 4A27	⚺ 1A39		∠ 1A50	☌ 6A45			⚹ 1S04			△ 3S02	☌ 6S24	□ 5S39								
♅				☌ 6A29	∠ 1A35	□ 1S06	☌ 5A06	△ 5S36		□ 1S40		⚹ 0S16	⚺ 1S01	☌ 2S11				△ 8A28	△ 4A07		⚺ 0A53
♆						△ 4S36	⚺ 1A36			△ 5S10		□ 3S46	☌ 4S31			☌ 5A03	☍ 5A03		□ 0A37	☌ 2A10	☌ 2S37
♇			☌ 4A58	⚺ 1A21			⚺ 0S03		☌ 6S42						□ 1A41	⚹ 3A24	△ 3A24	□ 3A19	⚻ 1S02	⚹ 0A31	
⚷	∠ 1A47			☍ 0S50		□ 6A45	☍ 0A34				△ 9A18	△ 5A55		☍ 7A50	△ 1S10			⚹ 2S48	⚹ 1A33	⚻ 0S00	
⚶									∠ 0A09		⚼ 2A14				△ 6A47	□ 5A03	□ 5A03				
⚴	□ 5S40	△ 8S28	□ 3A06	△ 6A43	□ 3S23	∠ 0S42	△ 8A07			∠ 0S08				⚼ 0A23	☍ 6A24			☌ 4A45	△ 9A06		
⚵			☌ 5S44				⚺ 0S43		☌ 5A57						□ 2S26		△ 4S10	□ 4S04	⚻ 0A17	⚹ 1S16	⚹ 3A30
⚳	△ 8S15		⚹ 0A31	□ 4A08			□ 5A32									△ 2A05	⚹ 2A05			△ 4A58	△ 9A45
☊	△ 5S49	□ 3S01						☌ 0S18	□ 3A45		☍ 1A40			△ 3A08		⚼ 1S09	∠ 1S09		△ 9A25		
☋		□ 3S01			△ 8S06			☍ 0S18	□ 3A45		☌ 1A40	△ 5A02		⚹ 3A08		∠ 1S09	⚼ 1S09				
As		∠ 0A00		⚹ 0A11			⚹ 1A35	∠ 2A43				☌ 6A57			△ 0A08	□ 1A52	□ 1A52	⚹ 1A47	☍ 2A34	□ 1A01	□ 5A48
Mc		⚼ 2A28	△ 0A58	⚻ 2A39	△ 7A26			∠ 0A15			⚼ 2A13				⚻ 2A20	☍ 0A36	☌ 0A36	⚺ 0A41	□ 5A02	☍ 3A29	☍ 8A16
⊗		△ 7A06				⚹ 0A08			△ 0A20	⚹ 0A26	⚻ 2A25	□ 0A57	☍ 0A12	⚻ 0A57			☌ 9A46		□ 5A20	☍ 6A53	☍ 2A06
⚸	⚼ 2A54			☌ 0A17			☌ 1A41							☌ 8A57	⚹ 0S03		⚻ 1S46	△ 1S41	△ 2A40	⚺ 1A07	

In this synastry grid, Bill Gates is across and Microsoft is down.

- Trine Suns △ ☉ show a smooth and effortless flow of energy around identity. As a presentation of the self, these two—Bill and his company—are of one mind and mission.
- Conjunct Moons ☌ ☽ tell us that these two charts speak the same language in the passion and creativity they inspire. Individually and together, these two are pioneering and futuristic.
- With trining Venuses △ ♀, money flows!
- Those trining Mars △ ♂ show an equal growth and sharing of power.

Next we look at the aspects between the personal planets and the outer planets. In Astrology, the outer planets represent longer cycles or trends of prosperity, of increase and decrease, and of societal structures. The aspects between the personal and the outer planets give us insights into how the respective entities—here, Bill Gates and Microsoft—relate to the outside world in the context of global business, the workaday world, and community issues. Here, too, we would expect to see strong connections if the company is to survive and thrive. And here, again, the symbiosis is incredible.

Both Jupiters ♃, the planet of abundance and luck, are making aspects to both personal and outer planets. This is significant for the mutual ability of these two to materialize those qualities. Microsoft prospers under Bill's leadership, and Bill flourishes in Microsoft's prosperity. Let's look at these aspects as an example.

Microsoft's Jupiter ♃ is ...

- ☾ In opposition ☍ to Bill's Moon ☽, creating potential conflict with Bill's emotional drive.
- ☾ Conjunct ☌ Bill's Mars ♂, with the mutual *yang* energies of these two planets supporting each other.
- ☾ Sextile ✶ Bill's Uranus ♅, giving favorable support to his original and innovative ideas.

Bill's Jupiter ♃ is ...

- ☾ Sextile ✶ Microsoft's Mercury ☿, establishing the company as the medium through which he communicates his ideas to the world.
- ☾ Square ☐ Microsoft's Uranus ♅, presenting the challenge of progress through transformation. (And how many times have we seen Microsoft shift direction to re-create itself, responding to changing market dynamics or, shall we say, government pressures?)
- ☾ Trine △ Microsoft's Neptune ♆, allowing the company to bring Bill's visions into the reality of practical applications. Interestingly, Microsoft's products are themselves tools of vision—software applications that convert computer code into recognizable images and functions.

The aspects with all of the outer planets and the personal planets for Bill and Microsoft are very strong, and have the resiliency to last through the years. Saturn ♄, the planet of discipline and longevity, influences focus and structure and the ability or inability of a company to develop products of lasting value and effect. We see Bill's Saturn trine

Microsoft's Venus ♄ △ ♀, showing the correlation between his hard work and the company's profits. We also see Microsoft's Saturn sextile Bill's Uranus ♄ ✳ ♅, applying the taskmaster planet's emphasis on hard work and perseverance to support Bill's entrepreneurial energy and innovative vision.

The aspects of Uranus ♅—the planet of new and futuristic events, sudden change, and the unexpected—reflect Microsoft's surprising rise to become a competitive force and leader within the high-tech industry. Who even dreamed that upstart Microsoft would surpass IBM and other industry giants? No one but its relentless leader. Yet there is the heavenly evidence, right there in the synastry grid: Uranus trine Uranus ♅ △ ♅. The flow from idea to product and back to new-and-improved idea is as effortless as, well, breathing.

And Bill's visionary Neptune ♆ trines △ Microsoft's Sun ☉ and Mercury ☿, so *of course* we will all recognize that there's just no way we can live without the latest and greatest version of Microsoft software, even if the old one seems to work just fine. For its part, Microsoft's Neptune trines Bill's Jupiter ♆△♃, ensuring that the visions he shares with us through the products Microsoft makes and sells will continue to generate good fortune—and dazzling fortunes—for them both.

Perhaps the most influential of the outer planet aspects is Bill's Pluto ♇, which trines △ Microsoft's Neptune ♆ and squares □ its Uranus ♅. Through Microsoft, Bill Gates has transformed—and will continue to transform—the world. Sure, that Pluto square Uranus ♇ □ ♅ has put some hills in the road. But 10 years ago Bill's mantra, "a personal computer on every desk," seemed a grandiose dream. Today, a desk *without* a personal computer is a nightmare. Bill Gates and Microsoft don't run the world, but together they have changed the way the world runs.

These two—the man and his company—enjoy a symbiotic relationship that we have to say really does look like it was made in Heaven. Most relationships are lucky to have 10 or 12 aspects. Among their personal planets and outer planets, Bill and Microsoft have an astonishing 33 aspects! Can you find them all? Write your counts at the corresponding aspects:

_____	Conjunctions ♂	_____	Trines △
_____	Sextiles ✳	_____	Quincunxes ⚻
_____	Squares □	_____	Oppositions ☍

Did you find them all? Here's our tally: 8 ♂, 4 ✳, 5 □, 12 △, 0 ⚻, and 4 ☍.

Synastry on the Charts

Now, let's see where the planets reside in the astrological houses of Bill's and Microsoft's birth charts. This gives us a different perspective of the same information we explored using the synastry grid.

As you look at this summary of information about Bill and Microsoft, look into their birth charts to practice finding the placements there. (Turn back to Chapter 3 to review Bill's birth chart.) You'll need to locate these planets when you prepare this information to explore *your* birth chart in relation to your company or job. The Tarot lets you explore connections through metaphor and imagery, so we've included an affiliated Major Arcana card for each astrological sign.

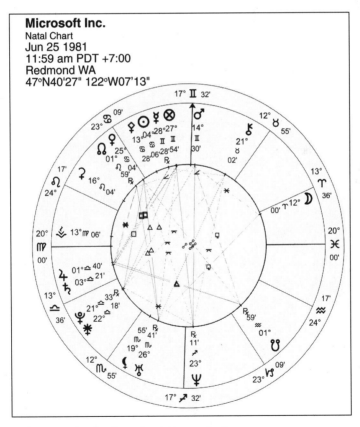

The noon birth chart for Microsoft, Inc.

Planet	Bill Gates Astro Sign	Energy	Astro House	Microsoft Astro Sign	Energy	Astro House
Sun ☉ (identity)	Scorpio ♏ Judgement	Water Fixed	5th (creativity)	Cancer ♋ Temperance	Water Cardinal	10th (career)
Moon ☽ (passion)	Aries ♈ Emperor	Fire Cardinal	10th (career)	Aries ♈ Emperor	Fire Cardinal	7th (partnership)
Mercury ☿ (communication)	Libra ♎ Justice	Air Cardinal	4th (home)	Gemini ♊ Lovers	Air Mutable	10th (career)
Venus ♀ (money)	Scorpio ♏ Judgement	Water Fixed	5th (creativity)	Cancer ♋ Temperance	Water Cardinal	11th (mission)
Mars ♂ (personal power)	Libra ♎ Justice	Air Cardinal	4th (home)	Gemini ♊ Lovers	Air Mutable	9th (beliefs)
Jupiter ♃ (prosperity)	Leo ♌ Strength	Fire Fixed	3rd (communication)	Libra ♎ Justice	Air Cardinal	1st (self)
Saturn ♄ (longevity)	Scorpio ♏ Judgement	Water Fixed	5th (creativity)	Libra ♎ Justice	Air Cardinal	1st (self)
Uranus ♅ (originality)	Leo ♌ Strength	Fire Fixed	1st (self)	Scorpio ♏ Judgement	Water Fixed	3rd (communication)
Neptune ♆ (vision)	Libra ♎ Justice	Air Cardinal	4th (home)	Sagittarius ♐ Chariot	Fire Mutable	4th (home)
Pluto ♇ (transformation)	Leo ♌ Strength	Fire Fixed	3rd (communication)	Libra ♎ Justice	Air Cardinal	2nd (values)

The Sun ☉ signs of these two—Bill's Scorpio ♏ and Microsoft's Cancer ♋—harmonize through their shared Element, Water. And remember from the synastry grid, these Suns form a trine △—smooth, flowing energy (like water!) that unites their goals and identities in good fortune and success. Bill and Microsoft share the same Moon ☽ sign, the Cardinal, catalytic Fire sign Aries ♈. The passions and emotions of one support the intensity and drive of the other, endlessly. It's important for the distribution of Elements in other areas of their charts to balance this, so let's take a look at how that works.

Element	Key Traits	Supportive	Conditional (Compatible/ Incompatible)	Challenging
Fire	Initiates, leads, competes, acts	Fire + Air	Fire + Fire Fire + Water	Fire + Earth
Earth	Focuses, grounds, directs, stabilizes	Earth + Water	Earth + Earth Earth + Air	Earth + Fire
Air	Balances, thinks, presents, envisions	Air + Fire	Air + Air Air + Earth	Air + Water
Water	Creates, feels, intuits, expresses	Water + Earth	Water + Water Water + Fire	Water + Air

The Fire + Fire combination between the respective Moons ☽ of Bill and Microsoft becomes supportive because it exists in the Moon's watery arena of emotion and passion. Here, Aries ♈ makes steam energy to fuel the emotional Moon. The Moon's Aries ♈ Fire stimulates action in Bill's 10th house of career and in Microsoft's 7th house of partnership, defining the ways in which both generate success for each. Amazingly, this is the only Fire + Fire placement in these two charts, and it's the only placement that can truly keep this Elemental combination endlessly supportive.

Let's look at another example: money, the purview of Venus ♀. Here we see the planet of resources in the Water signs of Scorpio ♏ in the 5th house of creativity for Bill, and of Cancer ♋ in the 11th house of mission for Microsoft. This establishes Water + Water, a conditional combination. Is it compatible or incompatible?

Bill has three planets in Water signs in his 5th house: Sun ☉, Venus ♀, and Saturn ♄. These are his planets of self, money, and longevity. Venus is the only planet in the 11th house of mission in either chart. Microsoft's mission is to make money through the flow of innovative ideas from Bill, ideas that generate the products that are the company's purpose for existing. This flow—of ideas from Bill and money to and from Microsoft—is going to continue for a long, long time. We can distill this to three concepts:

- ☯ Elemental combination: Water + Water
- ☯ Elemental key traits: creates + expresses
- ☯ Elemental nature: compatible

For Bill Gates and Microsoft, we found the following Elemental relationships.

Planet	Elemental Combination	Elemental Key Traits	Elemental Nature
Sun ☉ (*identity*)	Water + Water	Creates + expresses	Conditional/ compatible
Moon ☽ (*passion*)	Fire + Fire	Initiates + acts	Conditional/ compatible
Mercury ☿ (*communication*)	Air + Air	Envisions + presents	Conditional/ compatible
Venus ♀ (*money*)	Water + Water	Creates + expresses	Conditional/ compatible
Mars ♂ (*personal power*)	Air + Air	Thinks + envisions	Conditional/ compatible
Jupiter ♃ (*prosperity*)	Fire + Air	Leads + envisions	Supportive
Saturn ♄ (*longevity*)	Water + Air	Intuits + thinks	Challenging
Uranus ♅ (*originality*)	Fire + Water	Initiates + expresses	Conditional/ compatible
Neptune ♆ (*vision*)	Air + Fire	Envisions + acts	Supportive
Pluto ♇ (*transformation*)	Fire + Air	Leads + thinks	Supportive

To round out the picture for Bill and Microsoft, let's compare their ascendants, descendants, and midheavens. These heavenly positions are always on the same house cusps, so their house influences remain constant. The ascendant (public image) influences the 1st house of self and identity, the descendant (how you relate to others) influences the 7th house of partnerships, and the midheaven (how you direct your work) influences the 10th house of career.

Astro Position	Bill Gates		Microsoft	
	Astro Sign	Energy	Astro Sign	Energy
Ascendant	Cancer ♋	Water	Virgo ♍	Earth
	Temperance	Cardinal	*Hermit*	Mutable
Descendant	Capricorn ♑	Earth	Pisces ♓	Water
	World	Cardinal	*High Priestess*	Mutable
Midheaven	Pisces ♓	Water	Gemini ♊	Air
	High Priestess	Mutable	*Lovers*	Mutable

We'll use Tarot to explore these match-ups. When we look at Temperance, the Tarot's Major Arcana card of transformation, representing Bill's Cancer ♋ ascendant, we see a winged, surreal figure standing in the water at the edge of a flowing river, pouring water from one chalice to another. Flowers grow in abundance on the bank, and a path leads from the river to the mountains and a distant sun that is a crown. Can you see Bill's public persona in this imagery?

Microsoft's midheaven in Gemini ♊, its path to manifesting its career, gives what might as well be a window into the company's operations! The flowing, synchronized energy of the Tarot's the Lovers shows us that this company needs partnerships and relationships for its growth and success, and it is willing to "dance the dance" to make that happen. The sun shines bright and full behind this card's ethereal deity, who appears to be blessing the earthly union of abundance and fertility below.

You get the picture ... so what do you see in the cards for the descendants?

Spotlight on You and the Company You Keep

Now it's your turn. You need your personal birth chart, plus a birth chart for the start date of your company or for your job.

A **company** comparison lets you look at how your personal energies integrate with the company's energies. It can help you see areas of potential growth and opportunity as well as challenge and limitation. It shows you how the company appears as an entity, making the relationship perspective more tangible. It presents a chance to look at the bigger picture of your career through your work, promotion possibilities, and different job opportunities with this one company. And it helps you to evaluate whether this company will reward your contributions to its growth by investing in your personal advancement. If you *are* your company (self-employed or the owner) or intend to be with the company for a big part of your career, use a company chart for your comparison.

For your company you can use the location, date, and time of (in order of preference):

- Incorporation or formal organization
- First day of business
- First tax filing
- First contract signed
- First paycheck received (Many companies, especially small businesses, frame a copy of this!)

A **job** comparison is a narrower focus. It lets you look at how your abilities and interests integrate with the job's requirements and tasks. You can see where you are a good match with your job, where you might need to develop skills if you want to stay in this job, and an overview of your earning potential. You might be able to get a sense for whether this is a stepping-stone, a dead end, a springboard ... or your place in the work world. If you work for a large company or see yourself staying in a particular job for a long time, use a job chart for your comparison.

For your job, you can use the location, date, and time of (choose the one that reflects your perception of when you started the job):

- When you signed a letter of offer or acceptance
- When you signed an employment contract
- When you accepted the job
- Your first day on the job
- Your first paycheck

When you become comfortable and confident with the analysis process, you can look at all three charts—you, your job, and your company. For now, though, we'll just compare two charts—your birth chart and the chart for either your company or your job, whichever you choose.

Begin by creating this table of your summary data. From your personal birth chart, fill in the appropriate information for each planet.

Use the review chart in the previous section to fill in the energy, and remember to write in the Tarot card below each sign. When you've completed all of the information from your birth chart, repeat the process for your company or job's chart.

Planet	Your			Your Job or Company		
	Astro Sign/ Tarot Card	Energy	Astro House	Astro Sign/ Tarot Card	Energy	Astro House
Sun ☉ (identity)	___	___	___	___	___	___
Moon ☽ (passion)	___	___	___	___	___	___
Mercury ☿ (communication)	___	___	___	___	___	___
Venus ♀ (money)	___	___	___	___	___	___
Mars ♂ (personal power)	___	___	___	___	___	___
Jupiter ♃ (prosperity)	___	___	___	___	___	___
Saturn ♄ (longevity)	___	___	___	___	___	___
Uranus ♅ (originality)	___	___	___	___	___	___
Neptune ♆ (vision)	___	___	___	___	___	___
Pluto ♇ (transformation)	___	___	___	___	___	___

Tally the number of Elements:

Fire: _____ Earth: _____ Air: _____ Water: _____
Are any Elements significantly dominant? Which one(s)?

_____

Now, analyze your Elemental combinations. Do you want to know how long you might stay with this company or in this job? Look at Saturn ♄, your planet of longevity. Want to assess your prospects for growth, promotion, and advancement? Look at Mars ♂, your planet of personal power. Record your summaries here. The Elemental nature revealed will be either: compatible, conditional (compatible or incompatible depending on surrounding influences), or incompatible.

Planet	Elemental Combination	Elemental Key Traits	Elemental Nature
Sun ☉ (*identity*)	_____	_____	_____
Moon ☽ (*passion*)	_____	_____	_____
Mercury ☿ (*communication*)	_____	_____	_____
Venus ♀ (*money*)	_____	_____	_____
Mars ♂ (*personal power*)	_____	_____	_____
Jupiter ♃ (*prosperity*)	_____	_____	_____
Saturn ♄ (*longevity*)	_____	_____	_____
Uranus ♅ (*originality*)	_____	_____	_____
Neptune ♆ (*vision*)	_____	_____	_____
Pluto ♇ (*transformation*)	_____	_____	_____

Compare how you and your company's or job's ascendants, descendants, and midheavens match up. Write your name above the left columns and your company's name or job title over the right columns. From the beginning of the chapter or from your chart, fill in your significant signs and their energies (including the Tarot card associated with the sign). When you're done, do the same for your company or job.

Astro Position	You Astro Sign/ Tarot Card	Energy	Your Job or Company Astro Sign/ Tarot Card	Energy
Ascendant (*public self*)	_____	_____	_____	_____
Descendant (*connections with others*)	_____	_____	_____	_____
Midheaven (*approach to career*)	_____	_____	_____	_____

From your Tarot deck, pull the Major Arcana cards that associate with each astrological sign. Start with your ascendant and pair the Tarot cards that represent you and your company or job. Explore the imagery of the card that represents your ascendant. Does it reflect the public self, or persona, that you present on the job? Is this a different persona than the one you present in other public settings? How? Study the card and write your perceptions:

My Ascendant: _____

Tarot card: _____

Reflects who I am at work in these ways: _____

_____

Next, study the card that represents your company's or job's ascendant. Does it seem to accurately reflect how you, and others, perceive the company or position? Do you, as an employee, have a different perception than do customers or clients? Does the card reflect this? Study the card and write your perceptions:

Company/Job Ascendant: _____

Tarot card: _____

Reflects company/job in these ways: _____

_____

Look at the two cards together. What do you see? What story does this tell? Do the cards look like they belong together or like they have nothing in common? Explore the two cards' synergy and write your perceptions:

Seeing the cards for the ascendants together makes me think:

_____

_____

Pull the two Tarot cards for your respective descendants and reflect on the one for you. Does it represent how you connect and interact with others in the workplace? Do you prefer groups or to work alone? Does the card's image accurately characterize this? Study the card and write your perceptions:

My Descendant: _____

Tarot card: _____

Reflects how I relate to others at work in these ways:

_____

_____

Next, study the card that represents your company's or job's descendant. Does it seem to accurately reflect your company's or your job's expectations and requirements for how work groups and co-workers interact in the workplace? How so or why not? Examine the card and write your perceptions:

Company/Job Ascendant: _____

Tarot card: _____

Reflects company/job expectations for co-worker and work group relationships in these ways: _____

_____

Look at the two cards together. What do you see? What story does this tell? Do the cards look like they belong together or like they have nothing in common? Explore the two cards and write your perceptions:

Seeing the cards for the descendants together makes me think:

_____

_____

Pull the two Tarot cards for your respective midheavens and look at the one for you. Does it represent how you approach work goals and career objectives? Study the card and write your perceptions:

My Midheaven: _____

Tarot card: _____

Reflects my approach to work goals and career objectives in these ways: _____

_____

Next, study the card that represents your company's or job's midheaven. Does it support your approach, goals, and objectives? Examine the card and write your perceptions:

Company/Job Midheaven: _____

Tarot card: _____

Reflects how my company/job supports (or fails to support) my approach to my work goals and career objectives in these ways:

_____

_____

Look at the two cards together. What do you see? What story does this tell? Do the cards look like they belong together or like they have nothing in common? Explore the two cards and write your perceptions:

Seeing the cards for the midheavens together makes me think:

_____

_____

To complete your exploration through Astrology's synastry of the relationship that exists between you and your company or job, you need a synastry grid prepared from your birth charts. An astrologer can generate one for you. See Appendix A for more information on obtaining synastry grids.

Once you have the grid in hand, begin to identify the aspects between planets to discover favorable or challenging relationships. List the total number of each type of aspect you see in your synastry grid:

____ Conjunctions ♂, focus, shared energy

____ Sextiles ✶, favorable

____ Squares □, challenging, pushes for change

____ Trines △, ease, extremely favorable

____ Quincunxes ⚻, no shared energy, nothing in common

____ Oppositions ☍, difficulty, extremely challenging

So is this job or company a keeper? Or is it time to make a change in your job description, or even move on? Look at the specific planetary aspects to gain more clues to your compatibility on the job, as you explore the ways in which you can grow your job experience to best fulfill your lifework—work that not only gets you through the day, but leaves you eager to get back on the job tomorrow!

chapter 6

Failure Is a Fool's Opportunity

Devil or Fool? It's up to you!
Riding the cycles of the Moon ☽
Astrological transits, progressions, and retrogrades
Are you working in a void?
Tarot's Celtic Cross: answers and timing
Inviting intuition with Maneki Neko

Things go wrong sometimes. We know this comes as no surprise to you now, although often the events and circumstances that go wrong catch you by surprise when they happen. How you respond and what actions you take can determine the future of your job ... and your career, or at least your current work situation. The Intuitive Arts—Astrology, Tarot, and Psychic Intuition—can give you insights into why things go wrong and what you can do to turn challenging situations into opportunities.

Sooner or Later, Everybody Plays the Fool

Even when you love your job, tensions and problems arise that can make you feel chained, constrained, and at the mercy of circumstances—like Tarot's Devil. Too much work, not enough work. Office gossip. "It's not *my* job," which then *makes* it your job. Deadlines, budgets, meetings, and more meetings. Priorities (someone else's) that shift like sand at the ocean's edge. A boss who monitors your every move, a boss who doesn't even know your name. The same people out sick (again) and the same person (you) picking up the slack. Can you even bear another day of it? Some days, it seems not.

Tarot's Fool lifts his eyes to the sky. With feet about to step off a cliff! He (or she) looks like there's not a reason on earth—or in the heavens—to worry. Just for a minute, indulge yourself. Put yourself in this picture. Now it's you, off on some grand adventure. No one's asking, "Where's that report?" Rolling his or her eyes when you say you need one more day. Or breaking into hysterical laughter when you put in your vacation request. It's just you, your satchel of opportunity, and no limits. Ah, isn't this nice?

Can you turn the Tarot's repressive Devil into the devil-may-care Fool?

Moon ☽ Shadow …

The Moon ☽ does more than just light up the night. This heavenly body exerts powerful gravitational influences on her home planet, our Earth. Some say that the same magnetic tension that causes the seas to rise and fall subtly shifts the human body's biochemical balances. Physically and metaphorically, the Moon ☽ unites us with the cycles of our environment, affecting nature and all that it supports—including us.

The Moon ☽ has the shortest orbit of the planetary bodies. Its influence affects many dimensions of everyday life, none so significantly as communication. The Moon is the mother of emotions—passion, spontaneity, enthusiasm, imagination, ambition, sensitivity, warmth. Of course, the flip side of these powerful feelings can manifest as well—moodiness, impulse, fervor, fallacy, ruthlessness, brashness, sentimentality.

Face On, Face Off: Moon ☽ Cycles

We watch the cycles of the Moon ☽ in the night sky, moving through the stages of New Moon, Waxing Moon (first quarter), Full Moon, and Waning Moon (third quarter) every 29¹/₂ days, or roughly once a month. The first half of the Moon's cycle is when the Moon appears to be growing; this is a time to sow the seeds of opportunity. It culminates with the Full Moon. During the second half of the Moon's cycle, the Moon appears to be shrinking; this is a time to rest, recuperate, and prepare for the next cycle of growth. The Balsamic, or Dark Moon, anchors the nadir of the lunar cycle when the night sky is completely dark.

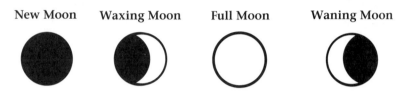

New Moon   Waxing Moon   Full Moon   Waning Moon

The Moon's energy moves from supportive and extrinsic during its waxing phase (New to Full), to reflective and intrinsic during its waning phase (Full to Balsamic).

The New Moon advances a sliver at a time to gently energize ideas and opportunities. It is hard, looking into the night sky, to distinguish the point at which the ending cycle's Balsamic Moon becomes the starting cycle's New Moon, but there's no question that you can feel it. Everyone—and everything—seems to awaken. Do you belong to any networking groups or organizations? Are you looking for a new job? Your efforts are more likely to succeed when initiated during the New Moon. Get out and about during this lunar phase. Pass out business cards, make new contacts, renew existing business relationships, establish plans, and schedule interviews. Starting a new business? Choose the New Moon as your start date to maximize fertile energy. The Waxing Moon (first quarter) tells you this cycle of initiation and growth has reached its halfway point.

The Full Moon marks the apex of the lunar cycle, when the Moon shines its round, bright light. The Moon's light and energy peak intensifies feelings and emotions. The Full Moon marks the time of harvest, when you reap the benefits of your efforts sown during the New and Waxing Moon phases. Full Moon glow brings clarity, which can illuminate your successes and invite others to share in the joy you feel, like Tarot's 4 of Wands. You might get news of a new job, promotion, account, contract, or other business success during the Full Moon.

Like Tarot's Ace of Wands, the New Moon heralds the energy of beginnings, growth, and fertile ideas, while the Page of Wands delivers their potential with the Waxing Moon.

But the illumination can be harsh as fluorescent lighting, too. The Full Moon encourages us to express the extremes of emotion, and people tend to "tell it like it is." Reactions and responses can catch you by surprise and, like Tarot's 5 of Wands, you can find yourself fighting instead of celebrating. The Full Moon escalates tensions that might exist because of office politics, changes in the business cycle, and incompatibilities that require effort to accommodate. If you have Fire signs in your work group, this is the time they are most likely to flare.

The energy of the Full Moon brings out the best, like Tarot's 4 of Wands, and the worst, like the 5 of Wands.

During the second half of the Moon's cycle, the Moon appears to be growing smaller—and so, for the time being, are opportunities. They're still there, of course, but they seem distant and moving away from you—like Tarot's 3 of Wands, you might feel you're watching your ship sail away rather than come in. You might find your efforts thwarted by events and circumstances that seem beyond your control, or by just outright moodiness as people tend to turn inward and introspective during the Waning Moon (third quarter) phase. This is a time of rest and restoration, to plow the ground in preparation for planting. Wrap up loose ends, close out details, clean up leftover responsibilities. Follow up on plans you put in place during the Waxing Moon, but hold off if you can on new ventures.

Tarot's 3 of Wands shows opportunity that, like the Waning Moon, seems to grow smaller and more distant. Like the Balsamic Moon, Tarot's King of Wands watches and waits, secure in the wisdom that his kingdom flourishes.

The Balsamic Moon marks the nadir of the lunar cycle, the point at which the Moon is totally dark. Now it seems *nothing* happens no matter how hard you prod and nag. But rest assured, much goes on behind the scenes during introspective time. If you're waiting for news about a job, promotion, or raise, check an astrological calendar before making that "I haven't heard from you yet …" call. If it's a Balsamic Moon, give it another day or two.

In nature, balsam is a soothing, medicinal salve made from the thick, dark resin of the balsa fir. Pungent and oily, it encourages healing by creating a protective barrier that focuses the body's own therapeutic energy inward. The Balsamic Moon similarly focuses energy inward. Its darkness quiets and calms chaos and confusion, like night encourages rest and sleep. This phase is a good time to reflect on desires, goals, and objectives.

Lunar Loops: Moon ☽ Transits

As the Moon ☽ moves through the Zodiac, it influences your emotions, moods, creativity, and intuition. It has the strongest affect on your personal Moon ☽ sign, which reflects your inner self and the way you express yourself. The Moon transits a different astrological sign about every two days; an astrological calendar can tell you the Moon's transits for the year in advance. Because the Moon ☽ is the natural ruler of the astrological sign Cancer ♋, when your Moon sign is Cancer you'll feel a magnified effect when the Moon transits this sign and its house placement in your birth chart.

Tarot's Moon represents the pull of emotional energy.

Moon ☽ In	Element	Beneficial	Challenging	Good Time To
Aries ♈ *Emperor*	Fire	Motivated, energized	Impatient	Start new assignments or make major changes
Taurus ♉ *Hierophant*	Earth	Calm, slowed	Stubborn	Return to work already underway
Gemini ♊ *Lovers*	Air	Receptive	Irrational	Write letters and reports, make phone calls
Cancer ♋ *Temperance*	Water	Sensitive, intuitive	Insecure	Reach out to others through activities that require or foster personal connections
Leo ♌ *Strength*	Fire	Creative, generous	Arrogant	Collaborate with others
Virgo ♍ *Hermit*	Earth	Organized, structured	Rigid	Focus on details and paperwork

Moon ☽ In	Element	Beneficial	Challenging	Good Time To
Libra ♎︎ *Justice*	Air	Cooperative, balanced	Hesitant	Initiate collaborations, sign partnership agreements
Scorpio ♏︎ *Judgement*	Water	Assertive, ambitious	Abrasive	Request resources (including a raise!)
Sagittarius ♐︎ *Chariot*	Fire	Progressive, open-minded	Reckless	Explore new interests and methods
Capricorn ♑︎ *World*	Earth	Persistent, diligent	Narrow-minded	Focus effort on financial and success goals
Aquarius ♒︎ *Star*	Air	Innovative, selfless	Flighty	Brainstorm new ideas, make intellectual connections
Pisces ♓︎ *High Priestess*	Water	Artistic, visionary	Fearful	Strategize and conceptualize

Use an Astrology calendar to look up today's Moon ☽ transit. Do the Elements of your Moon ☽ sign and the day's Moon transit support or challenge one another? You're more likely to encounter the challenging side of the Moon's influence when the Elements are challenging. Then look at the Tarot cards for your Moon sign and the day's Moon transit. What does your Psychic Intuition tell you when you look at the two Tarot cards and the day's planned activities? You can create a Moon ☽ transit journal, or jot the basics in your day planner to help remind you of the day's supports and challenges.

If your personal Moon ☽ sign is in the Water sign Pisces ♓︎, Judgement's visionary flow will manifest as epiphanies of the Hermit's internal truth during transiting Virgo ♍︎ Moons ☽.

May the Force Be with You: Eclipses

Eclipses occur when the Sun ☉ or the Moon ☽ crosses the path of the other luminary, temporarily obscuring it from view. It's a solar eclipse when the Moon blocks the Sun, and a lunar eclipse when the Sun blocks the Moon. We usually have two of each in a calendar year. Astrologically, eclipses intensify the current energies—the solar eclipse more than the lunar. But you have to focus this intensity through your intentions and efforts.

When a solar eclipse falls in a house, it illuminates that house. A solar eclipse that falls in the 6th house of work, for example, shines the spotlight on events in the workplace. A lunar eclipse heightens emotional issues in whatever house it falls. When a lunar eclipse falls in your 10th house of career, you might find yourself in a contemplative, intrinsic evaluation of your career and career goals.

An astrological calendar tells when and in what sign eclipses take place. To determine how you can make best use of the eclipse, find the sign of the eclipse on your wheel of houses. The house the sign rules is where you'll feel the eclipse.

Orbits of Influence

As all of the planets follow their orbits, they travel through the 12 astrological signs and houses. Like the Moon ☽, each stimulates the sign and house it visits. Each planet also makes aspects with other planets, affecting their energies. A planet's most intense energy comes when it transits its natural sign, and focuses this energy in the house where that sign resides. A second area of focus beams to the house that the planet naturally rules.

For example, Mercury ☿, the planet of communication, rules Virgo ♍, the natural sign of the 6th house of work. If your natal Mercury falls in your 6th house in your birth chart, then when Mercury transits you're going to get a double-espresso jolt supporting your ability to express yourself in the work arena. You'll shine at presentations, in meetings, and for job interviews. If Mercury is in another house on your birth chart, then you'll get a single-espresso jolt to that house and more like a cup-of-coffee buzz to your 6th house when Mercury visits Virgo ♍.

How often a planet visits an astrological sign depends on the length of its orbit. The personal planets—Sun ☉, Moon ☽, Mercury ☿, Venus ♀, and Mars ♂—are the most frequent houseguests, having the shortest orbits. The outer planets—Jupiter ♃, Saturn ♄, Uranus ♅, Neptune ♆, and Pluto ♀—don't visit as often but stay longer and have a more intense affect. They have a larger sphere of influence, shaping the social conscience and general mission of entire generations. As the outer planets move more slowly, their transits mark signpost experiences during your life cycle, such as midlife, unlike the Moon ☽ where new transits start every couple of days.

Planet	Rules the Astro Sign(s)	Work Influences	Transits Each Astro Sign
Sun ☉	Leo ♌	Personal presentation, will to succeed, physical strength and appearance	Every year
Moon ☽	Cancer ♋	Emotions, moods, creativity, intuition	Every 29½ days
Mercury ☿	Gemini ♊ and Virgo ♍	Thinking, logic, reason, writing, books, computers, speaking, media	Every year
Venus ♀	Taurus ♉ and Libra ♎	Money, resources, material possessions, partnerships	Every year
Mars ♂	Aries ♈ and Scorpio ♏	Energy, passion, ambition, stamina, achievement, courage	Every 2 years
Jupiter ♃	Sagittarius ♐ and Pisces ♓	Fortune, wealth, luck, intellect, higher education, travel	Every 12 years
Saturn ♄	Capricorn ♑ and Aquarius ♒	Hard work, discipline, responsibility, limits, structure, attention to detail, perseverance, delay, karma	Every 28 to 30 years
Uranus ♅	Aquarius ♒	Originality, invention, rebellion, free will	Every 84 years
Neptune ♆	Pisces ♓	Illusion, insight, awareness, spirituality	Every 165 years
Pluto ♀	Scorpio ♏	Destruction and rebuilding, rebirth, transformation	Every 248 years

Some transit influences are extraordinarily supportive for career matters. When Jupiter ♃ or Venus ♀ visits your 6th house of work, it's the astrological equivalent of Tarot's 9 of cups—the Wish Card. Wondering if you're going to get that raise? Venus ♀ in your 2nd house of money or in Taurus ♉, the 2nd house's natural sign, tips the odds in your favor. At the very least, it won't hurt to make sure the boss knows of your outstanding effort and contributions, as rewards of value come in many different packages.

Planetary transits can make you feel nothing is beyond your reach, like Tarot's 9 of Cups ... or, as in the 9 of Swords, that it's too much to even get out of bed.

Other transits make you want to stay in bed all day with the covers pulled over your head. Transits that create squares □ and oppositions ☍ to your 6th and 10th houses in your birth chart can encumber even the simplest tasks with difficulty and challenge, leaving you feeling like Tarot's 9 of Swords. Maybe Venus ♀ in Taurus ♉ squares □ Saturn ♄ in Capricorn ♑, pitting the bull against the goat in a classic celestial confrontation. You might get your raise, but first you'll have to convince your boss that you're worth it ... and it might be smaller than you hoped.

Celestial Challenges: One Step Forward, Two Steps Back?

Planetary transits can appear to be moving forward (direct), standing still (stationary), or moving backward (retrograde). We say "appear" because of course planets always move in the same direction along their orbits; it just looks like they change direction from our vantage point here on Earth.

- **Direct transit.** The normal movement of the planets is counter-clockwise through the Zodiac, and a planet that is direct gives the appearance of moving forward. The influence of a direct transit is straightforward; the planet exerts the energies of its natural characteristics.

- **Stationary transit.** A planet goes stationary, or appears to stand still, when it is switching from direct to retrograde or from retrograde to direct. A stationary planet exerts intensely focused energy, heightening the effect of its natural characteristics.

- **Retrograde transit.** A planet that is retrograde appears to be moving clockwise, or backward. This is one appearance that is all about deception, as nothing is what it seems during a retrograde transit, which can signal delays or challenges.

Some astrological influences are outright challenging, no way around it. Like squares □, they can bring struggle and confrontation. But they also offer tremendous opportunity to make the best manifestation of talents and abilities.

Retrograde "Re" Action

Uh-oh … here comes trouble. Well, at least challenge. When a planet goes retrograde ℞, its energy becomes scattered instead of focused. Retrogrades can create chaos and havoc. But a retrograde also is a gift from the universe inviting you to engage in some "re" action—re-consider, re-think, re-align, re-schedule, re-claim. Like the halo that surrounds Tarot's Hanged Man, there is much good within this energy. Mercury ☿ is the most frequent retrograde, occurring about three times a year and lasting three to four weeks. Other planets retrograde less often but for longer periods of time, up to months.

Planet in Retrograde ℞	"Re" Action	Challenging Influences
Mercury ☿	Revise, refocus, reorganize	Communication, computers, technology, thinking, correcting misunderstandings and miscues
Venus ♀	Reevaluate, reconsider	Financial planning and management, resources allocation, correcting past mistakes in handling money

Planet in Retrograde ℞	"Re" Action	Challenging Influences
Mars ♂	Reassess, revisit	Completed work, goals, job and career plans, adjusting methods and approaches
Jupiter ♃	Review, redevelop	Professional growth and education, personal ethics and standards, returning to school or training
Saturn ♄	Redefine, reinforce	Daily job activities, work habits, foundations, discarding what has become outmoded or no longer effective
Uranus ♅	Rebel, reject	Tradition, customs, habits, status quo, investigating new paradigms
Neptune ♆	Reexamine, recommit	Spiritual connections, humanitarian efforts, sense of belonging to the larger family of the human race, exploring beliefs and philosophical foundations
Pluto ♇	Re-form, rebirth	Transformation, awareness of role and position in a larger picture, adjusting to life-altering events

You may have retrograde planets in your astrological birth chart. Their influence will carry a "re" energy of sometimes karmic significance. Look at your birth chart now. Do you see the retrograde ℞ symbol in any of your houses? If so, write the planet, sign, house, and challenging influences:

Retrograde ℞ Planet	Sign	House	Challenging Influences
_____	_____	_____	_____
_____	_____	_____	_____
_____	_____	_____	_____
_____	_____	_____	_____

Like Tarot's the Hanged Man, when planets go retrograde ℞ their energies are upended.

Watch Out for the Void of Course Moon ☽

Have you shown up for a staff meeting only to find out it was cancelled but no one let you know? Taken clients to your favorite restaurant for lunch hoping you could get in without a reservation and finding instead that the restaurant was closed for remodeling? Sent an e-mail telling co-workers you'd be out of the office Friday and Monday, only to return to find your e-mailbox overflowing with angry messages demanding to know why you're not responding? Submitted a report the day before it was due only to find out three days later that your boss doesn't remember seeing it and can't find it? These miscues have "void of course Moon" written all over them!

As the Moon ☽ moves through a sign, it creates aspects with other planets in your chart. These aspects are the Moon's course—its path of connection with other planetary bodies. When the Moon completes its final aspect during its stay within a sign, its course goes void—there's nothing left for it to do except continue its travel to the next sign. The time between the Moon's final aspect in one sign and its first aspect in the next sign is called a void of course Moon—an astrological "time-out" when there is no activity involving the Moon. A void can last from a few minutes to longer than a day. A void of course Moon is a good opportunity to retreat from externally focused activities and concentrate on work or tasks you've set aside because they need "quiet time." Astrological calendars note void of course Moons along with transits and moon cycles.

When Saturn ♄ Returns

Saturn ♄ is the planet of structure and foundations, and it revisits its birth location in your chart every 28 to 30 years. Saturn wants you to get your act together, to build the base that can and will support you in manifesting your talents and abilities. Saturn ensconces itself in a sign for about two and a half years, so there's no chance you're going to miss its influence. Saturn shines a matter-of-fact, pragmatic, and sometimes harsh light on your life, and what you see isn't always pretty or pleasant. But it does generate growth and change, and that's its purpose.

Saturn makes its returns to everyone at about the same age, at 28 to 30 years old the first time and 58 to 60 years old the second time. If you're blessed with a long life, you'll get a third visit from this cosmic taskmaster, when you're 88 to 90 years old. Saturn's visits cause all of us to look back on our jobs and careers, to ask ourselves, "Is my current job fulfilling enough to carry me toward my future career goals?" Often we have to answer, "Not really."

During Saturn's visits you might feel driven to add education to your experience, or return to finish a degree you put off to follow other opportunities. Your current career might seem dreary and old, causing you to look at a complete change of direction. Or you might like your current job and career path, but find that you now want to advance. Your perception of work and work ethics shifts. Saturn ♄ pushes you into a new dynamic of more experience or more expression of yourself through your work. How far you've come determines which way you'll take your new cycle of career growth and development.

Filmmaker Spike Lee hit the theme of his life at his Saturn ♄ return when he produced the film *Do the Right Thing* … precisely the right thing to make it clear he was ready and willing to manifest the potential inherent in his astrological birth chart. Spike's third film, *Do the Right Thing* established him as one of America's premier independent filmmakers. He's enjoyed a productive, although at times controversial, career. When we look at Spike's noon birth chart, we can see why.

With his Sun ☉, Venus ♀, and Mercury ☿ all in Pisces ♓ in his 10th house of career, and Pisces ♓ on his midheaven, Spike Lee's birth chart certainly lays the foundation for his creative talent to flow. Venus trines Uranus ♀ △ ♅ in his 2nd house, showing that this creativity will challenge conventions and traditions. Mars in his 12th house squares Pluto, the planet of transformation ♂ □ ♇. Not only will his work challenge us, but it will transform our beliefs and practices.

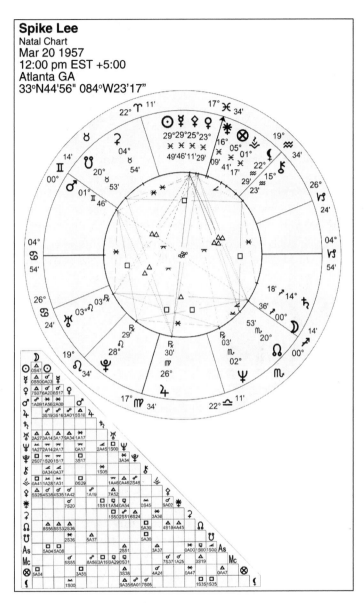

Birth chart of filmmaker Spike Lee.

Along with those powerful conjunctions of Sun ☉, Mercury ☿, and Venus ♀ in Spike's birth chart, a grand trine △ sets up a smooth flow of energy between his 10th house of career, his 2nd house of money and resources, and his 6th house of work. These major aspects gave him the perseverance and convincing communication skills to garner support for his ideas from those around him. Despite the celestial support, Spike's had his share of ups and downs. His wasn't an easy Saturn ♄ return but he remained focused, helping him to complete his career visions.

Expect Uranus ♅ to Bring the Unexpected

Sea changes and paradigm shifts are the hallmark of a Uranus ♅ return. Uranus transits the zodiac once every 84 years and stays about 7 years in each sign. Could this be the force behind the proverbial "seven-year itch?" Quite possibly! Not everyone experiences a full Uranus return, although we all feel its quarter-point influences. The most significant is the halfway point, which most people experience in their early to mid-40s. Those radical changes of midlife crisis often make perfect sense in the context of Uranus's influence, which challenges convention and tradition.

A Uranus ♅ return brings a jolt and the unexpected.

    What do *your* Saturn ♄ and Uranus ♅ returns say about *your* birth chart, and manifesting the best potential in the times of *your* life?

As the Wheel Rotates: Progressions

Another way to look at the influences of the planets is to do what astrologers call a progressed chart. While your birth chart captures a snapshot of the planetary positions at your birth, a progression presents a symbolic picture of the heavens at a particular point in your life. A progressed chart advances your Sun ☉ one day along the chart wheel for each year of your life. Unlike your birth chart, however, the cosmic configuration that your progressed chart reflects is not a permanent influence. It does what it says—shows your progress. It also shows whether you're moving toward or away from manifesting the potential and the lifework path of your birth chart. You can get a progressed chart from an astrologer, or consult Appendix A for websites where you can order charts.

Let's take a look at the birth and progressed charts of America's beloved poet, Maya Angelou. Her progressed chart looks at the time of her birthday in 2003, at age 75.

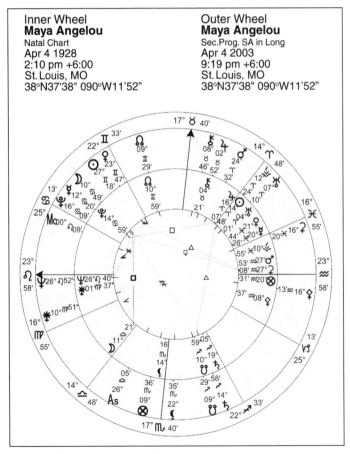

The birth and progressed charts of poet and educator Maya Angelou.

Here's a woman who has lived a full and varied life, literally working her way through many jobs to finally manifest her creative talents. From a natal ascendant Leo ♌, the Fixed Fire energy that supported Maya's pursuit of her creative calling, she now has progressed to Libra ♎ rising, focusing her public image in poetry, the arts, publishing, the media, and justice—all that we associate with this articulate and visionary woman. She will continue to work with the written, spoken, creative word until her progressed Sun ☉ enters Cancer ♋ within three years. Then Maya will experience yet another new focus on her work, career, and contributions to society as the Cancerian Water element comes forward to give a stronger, sharper focus on family, children, home, and culture.

When Arlene compares Maya's birth and progressed charts, she sees there is a good flow of energy as the Sun sextiles Neptune ☉ ✶ ♆, with another sextile from Venus ♀ in Gemini ♊ to Mars ♂ in Aries ♈. Maya will enjoy more work and more opportunities for projects both personal and public. Education and publishing will continue, too, as she continues to grow and fulfill her goals in her work and service to others.

Turning to Tarot for Answers and Timing

Whether you're looking for a new job or to make changes in your current job, Tarot's Celtic Cross is a wonderful reading for determining the likelihood and timing of events. The cards identify timing by suit:

- ☯ Wands represent the season of spring.
- ☯ Cups represent the season of summer.
- ☯ Swords represent the season of fall.
- ☯ Pentacles represent the season of winter.

The number on Minor Arcana cards identifies days, weeks, or months. We look at the number itself as well as its suit association. The 3 of Wands, for example, might suggest three days, weeks, or months from now depending on how long it is until spring. In the Major Arcana cards, the sign associated with the card can point to a time of year. The Magician, for example, is Aries ♈, which is spring. Major Arcana cards reflect longer times, often a year or more.

Tarot's Celtic Cross Spread has 10 cards, and here's how to interpret each one:

- ☯ **Card 1.** This is you. You can choose the card you'd like to represent you, or you can let the deck make the choice when you deal the cards. This is the first card of timing.

- **Card 2.** The cover card. It represents forces or energies that oppose you and your desires. This card always appears upright; so if you draw it reversed, turn it upright.

- **Card 3.** The foundation or source of your question. Why do you want to know what you've asked? You might be fearful about the future, uncertain whether you're making the right choice, concerned about your motivations. Sometimes this is the *real* question that you want to ask.

- **Card 4.** The immediate past related to your question. Have you received a job offer, applied for a new job, realized your boss is not supporting your career objectives? Although these events are history, they've shaped the direction you're now exploring.

- **Card 5.** The current energy surrounding you and the situation or event that you're questioning. This energy is simply present; you must take action to manifest it to support (or not) your question. This energy is total free will; it may or may not come to pass.

- **Card 6.** The energy of the event or situation that will manifest. This is what *will* happen; all that remains is for you to see what unfolds. This energy is already in motion, and this card tells you its eventual outcome. This is the second card of timing.

- **Card 7.** How you feel about the question you've asked. Are you afraid of failure ... or success? Does the job involve relocating or making a dramatic change in your lifestyle? Do you worry that you're not qualified or won't be able to meet expectations (yours or those of others)? This card shows you what you feel or fear so you can confront it and move on.

- **Card 8.** How others feel about or affect the outcome. Does your boss support your career plans? Is someone else pushing you, or trying to hold you back? In the work world, other people often make or break opportunities for you, so it pays to know your allies ... and your adversaries.

- **Card 9.** What must first take place for you to reach your desired outcome or goal. You might need to return to school, or work at an interim job. Sometimes this card identifies delays, and other times it just tells you what hoops you'll have to jump through to get what you want.

- **Card 10.** Final outcome. This card tells you what is going to happen with respect to your question. What comes before influences this result, but as long as you follow the path you've started on this will be the outcome. This is the third and final card of timing.

A Sample Celtic Cross Reading

Sawyer came to Arlene in December for a reading to find out whether she was likely to get hired on by a company she'd been working for on a contract basis. Sawyer's boss told her that she was sure to get hired as a permanent employee when her contract expired. Sawyer wanted to know when, so she knew whether to look for other work in the interim. What do you see in Sawyer's cards?

Sawyer's Celtic Cross Tarot reading to answer the question: "When will I get hired back?"

Your Celtic Cross Reading

What do *you* want to know about your job or career prospects and when they might become reality for you? Write your question here:

_____

_____

If you want to choose a card to represent you in the spread, do that now. Then concentrate on your question and shuffle your Tarot deck. When you're comfortable with the cards, draw one at a time and place each in its position.

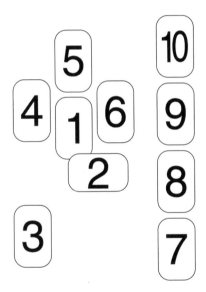

Write the name of the card and your interpretations here:

Card 1 (you): _____

Card 2 (cross): _____

Card 3 (foundation): _____

Card 4 (past): _____

Card 5 (present): _____

Card 6 (what will happen): _____

Card 7 (how you feel): _____

Card 8 (how others feel): _____

Card 9 (what must happen): _____

Card 10 (outcome): _____

Inviting Prosperity

Sometimes, even fortified with a knowledge of Astrology's transits, progressions, retrogrades, and void of course Moons, as well as insights from Tarot's revealing readings, the best way to turn challenging situations to beneficial opportunities is to go with your gut; that is, to access your Psychic Intuition. Trusting your intuition under less-than-perfect circumstances is a personal endeavor—one you can hone and develop by keeping an Intuition Journal. Start a notebook that has three columns, "Situation," "Gut Feeling Surrounding the Situation," and "Resolution." Keep track of how your intuition resonates to what happens on the work front and whether your intuitive responses are on- or off-track.

To let your work colleagues know that you are inviting positive energy and solutions into your office, consider placing the Japanese symbol of fortune, the cat Maneki Neko, in your office window or doorway. Depending on the appearance of the cat, Maneki Neko invites specific energies of prosperity. A golden cat, or one holding a coin, invites a strong financial return on investment. Maneki Neko raises a left paw to draw in clients and a right raised paw to draw in financial success. A Calico cat is good luck. What kind of beneficial energy does *your* office need to raise? May Maneki Neko welcome success in all your career endeavors!

chapter 7

A Work-Study Program for Lifelong Learning

Psychic Intuition climbs the pyramid of needs
Stay or go? Not always an obvious answer
Goddess power of the asteroids
Astrology's synastry: mastering challenge in business relationships
Cards of change, cards of chance: Tarot's Wheel of Fortune

You spend a good part of your life preparing for the work you expect will carry you through your career. You study and practice—you might go to college or technical school, complete an apprenticeship program, or make the most out of on-the-job training. So when you get a ways down the road and discover that you really don't like what you're doing, the job market is limited, or your line of work is fast becoming extinct, it's natural to feel a sense of confusion. How could something so right turn out so wrong? In a word, change. You change, the world around you changes. Sometimes we embrace these changes, and sometimes we fight them. But they take place anyway! Let the Intuitive Arts take you deeper into yourself, your needs, your desires so you can begin to craft the work that both sustains and satisfies you. In this chapter, you use your Psychic Intuition to climb the pyramid to self-actualization; Astrology to chart your mentoring, partnership, nurturing, and warrior wisdom potential in the Goddess power of the asteroids; and Tarot to spin the wheel of change and chance.

What You Want Is Really What You Need

When we start our journeys through the work world, our first jobs tend to be survival-oriented. All we want to do is keep a roof over our heads, food in the fridge, and clothes on our bodies. Then we start to acquire skills, knowledge, and experience. Others take notice, and we get promotions and raises. We start to care about where we work, the people we work with, the work we do—and what others think about us. We feel a sense of ownership, accountability, and pride. Finally, it becomes important to meet our personal needs for fulfillment and satisfaction, above and beyond basic survival. "A job" becomes "my career" becomes "my lifework."

Psychologist Abraham Maslow identified this progression as the hierarchy of needs, a dimension of human existence that plays out in each arena of our lives—work, family, love, home. Researchers tell us that when it comes to what we want from work—our jobs and our careers—five key factors define the difference between satisfaction and dissatisfaction. Not surprisingly, these factors parallel Maslow's hierarchy.

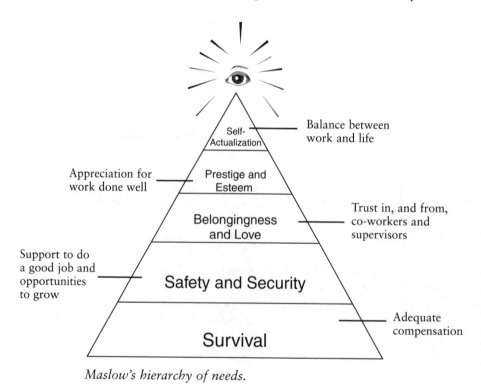

Maslow's hierarchy of needs.

The pyramid, chosen by Egyptian and Mayan cultures as the form for sacred structures, holds an enduring power base upon which to reach with confidence toward enlightenment. The Great Seal of the United States pictures such a pyramid on its reverse, with a Third Eye floating illuminated at its point. Over time, you will find yourself building many such pyramids in your quest to find and fulfill your life-work. Your existence, like the universe that supports it, is far from static! As you change and grow, your interests and needs change and grow. Your pyramid evolves with greater and deeper purpose.

Tarot Guides the Way

The Tarot's Major Arcana cards mark the journey of life and of your career quest. Each level of the pyramid has a corresponding Tarot card to lend its insights and energy as you travel your path.

The Fool takes the lead on the journey's first leg—Survival. This Aries ♈ energy steps forward with determination and confidence, representing you off to a strong start. New opportunities and endless possibilities await!

Strength represents your needs—Security. This Leo ♌ energy is fiercely protective, making it clear that when you have the resources your job requires you are there to do the best job you can do.

The Lovers represents your work group or partnership—Belonging. People make the difference in the workplace, and this Gemini ♊ energy is devoted to collaborative effort.

The Star represents your accomplishments and achievements—Prestige and Esteem. Everybody needs and wants recognition for work done well, and this Aquarius ♒ energy shines the spotlight on your efforts.

The World represents your satisfaction, happiness, and fulfillment—Self-Actualization. This grounded, focused Capricorn ♑ energy supports your sense of completion.

Your Personal Lifework Pyramid

How well does your current job or career lay a foundation for your lifework pyramid? In the following table, describe how your current job or career does and does not meet your needs. Then, draw upon your Psychic Intuition and meditate deeply upon the lifework pyramid as you explore your work as a master builder of enlightenment. For inspiration (and a nifty visual aid), hold a dollar bill in your hands and look into George Washington's eyes. Then, fold the dollar to the left and you will see the pyramid of the Great Seal. Use this wonderful symbol of abundance to remind you that all your dreams for your life-work are possible!

Need	Current Job or Career Meets in These Ways	Current Job or Career Fails to Meet in These Ways
Survival: *Adequate compensation*	_____	_____
Security: *Support to do a good job, opportunities to grow*	_____	_____
Belonging: *Trust in and from co-workers and supervisors*	_____	_____
Prestige and Esteem: *Appreciation for work done well*	_____	_____
Self-Actualization: *Balance between work and life*	_____	_____

When to Hold, When to Fold

When work conditions become untenable, it's time to decide what you're going to do about your situation. How long can you stay, hoping things will get better or that you can work things out? When do you make the break and move on? Has a downturn in your industry or downsizing in your company left you with no choice but to move on? In the following questions, check the one answer for each that best describes your current job situation. If you're presently between jobs, you can answer the questions for the job you held most recently.

Do you stay to work things out, like Tarot's 3 of Pentacles, or head for other opportunities, like the 8 of Cups?

1. Why do you have your present job?
   ___ It pays the bills.
   ___ It's the work I wanted to do or the company I wanted to work for.
   ___ The opportunity was there so I took it.
   ___ I thought it would be a good stepping-stone to the job I really want to have.

2. How did you get your current job?
   ___ Through someone I know or someone who works here.
   ___ Answered an ad, went through the interview process, got hired.
   ___ I was invited to apply for the job so I did, and here I am.
   ___ Through networking.

3. How long did it take you to get your current job?
   ___ Less than two weeks.
   ___ Between two weeks and two months.
   ___ Between two months and six months.
   ___ Longer than six months.

4. What do you like *best* about your current job?
   ___ The job's responsibilities and tasks.
   ___ My co-workers and work environment.
   ___ The pay and benefits.
   ___ The reaction I get when I tell people what I do and where I work.

5. What do you like *least* about your current job?

　　 ___ The job's responsibilities and tasks.

　　 ___ My co-workers and work environment.

　　 ___ The pay and benefits.

　　 ___ The reaction I get when I tell people what I do and where I work.

6. When you compared your birth chart to your company's or job's chart (refer to Chapter 5), how did your ascendant, descendant, and midheaven match up?

　　 ___ Mostly supportive Element combinations.

　　 ___ Mostly conditional Element combinations.

　　 ___ Mostly challenging Elemental combinations.

7. When you compared your birth chart to your company's or job's chart (refer to Chapter 5), how did your personal planets—Sun ☉, Moon ☽, Mercury ☿, Venus ♀, and Mars ♂—match up?

　　 ___ Mostly supportive Element combinations.

　　 ___ Mostly conditional Element combinations.

　　 ___ Mostly challenging Elemental combinations.

8. When you compared your birth chart to your company's or job's chart (refer to Chapter 5), how did your outer, or long-term, planets—Jupiter ♃, Saturn ♄, Uranus ♅, Neptune ♆, Pluto ♇—match up?

　　 ___ Mostly supportive Element combinations.

　　 ___ Mostly conditional Element combinations.

　　 ___ Mostly challenging Elemental combinations.

9. From your Tarot deck, pick one card that represents you in your current job. Then pick one card that represents you in your dream job. When you look at these two cards side by side, how do they appear to get along?

　　 ___ They go pretty good together.

　　 ___ The more I look at them, the more commonality I see.

　　 ___ Maybe over time, getting to know each other better ...

　　 ___ Talk about the ultimate odd couple!

10. If you're not working right now, why?

　　 ___ I was fired from my last job.

　　 ___ Company downsizing eliminated my last job.

____ I left my last job by my choice.

____ I'm new to the job market.

Do you find any surprises in your answers? Often you have a sense of what's out of balance but aren't quite sure of the specifics. Once you start to zero in, you can create a plan of action. Use the information you've learned from these questions to deepen your meditation practice. As you sit in meditation, using Yoga's lotus pose or a seated cross-legged pose, whatever is comfortable for you, feel your body become the base of your lifework pyramid and as you inhale feel the energy of your intent travel upward to the Third Eye of your forehead. As you relax and center, meditate upon your lifework goals. If you feel you are working on issues specific to any level of the pyramid, hold the corresponding Tarot card in your hand as you meditate, or put it under your pillow before you go to sleep to invite intuitive dream messages.

Additional Astrological Energy: The Asteroids

A belt of cosmic fragments follows a somewhat irregular orbit between Mars ♂ and Jupiter ♃, with some of them crossing the orbital paths of the two planets. Astrologers recognize this collection of asteroids and planetoids, first discovered in 1801 (barely yesterday, astrologically speaking), as the "Goddess belt" for their significant *yin* influences. Your astrological birth chart identifies the placements of four prominent asteroids—Ceres ⚳, Juno ⚵, Pallas Athene ⚴, and Vesta ⚶.

The powerful feminine energies of these heavenly bodies affect everyone, male or female. Like other planets, the asteroids have affiliations with astrological signs and Tarot Major Arcana cards.

Asteroid	Astro Signs	Influences
Ceres ⚳	Cancer ♋, Virgo ♍, Taurus ♉	Nurturing, mentoring, taking care of, cycles of growth
Juno ⚵	Libra ♎, Scorpio ♏	Long-term partnerships, relating to others
Pallas Athene ⚴	Leo ♌, Libra ♎, Aquarius ♒	Strength, "warrior wisdom," competition, the winner's circle
Vesta ⚶	Scorpio ♏, Virgo ♍	Power, allegiance, loyalty, fulfillment

As you look at the influences of these asteroids, do they seem familiar? When we look at them, we see the lifework pyramid of needs!

Asteroid	Level of Need	Tarot Card(s)
Ceres ⚳	Survival and Security *Adequate compensation,* *support to do a good job,* *opportunities to grow*	The Fool, Strength
Juno ⚵	Belonging *Trust in and from co-workers* *and supervisors*	The Lovers
Pallas Athene ⚴	Prestige and Esteem *Appreciation for work* *done well*	The Star
Vesta ⚶	Self-Actualization *Balance between work* *and life*	The World

The astrological houses in which these asteroids appear in your birth chart identify the ways you carry out each heavenly body's particular influences. The aspects these asteroids form in your birth chart determine the ways they affect your approaches to your job and your career. They can be supportive, like trines △ and sextiles ✳, or challenging, like oppositions ☍ and squares ☐.

Ceres ⚳: Taking Care of Business

In Roman mythology, Ceres ⚳ is the goddess of the crops—and her realm, the cycle of cultivation, from planting to harvest. When Ceres smiled on the Earth, abundance came. In your astrological birth chart, Ceres shows how you nurture, mentor, and take care of yourself and others—as well as how you prefer to have others do the same for you.

Ceres's natural affiliation with Earth signs Taurus ♉ and Virgo ♍ gives grounding to your approach. Ceres in your 6th house of work or your 10th house of career (on your midheaven) suggests that you enjoy work in which you give of yourself or take care of others. How this works out depends on the sign affiliation. Ceres in Aries ♈ is likely to be affectionate and demonstrative; Ceres in Gemini ♊ talkative and intellectual.

The Tarot's Major Arcana cards the Fool and Strength represent the mentoring, nurturing characteristics of Ceres ⚳.

Juno ⚵: Commitment

Juno ⚵ is the goddess of long-term relationships. Noted for her sense of fairness and fidelity, Juno bestows equity and longevity. In work and career she rules partnerships between people, and between people and companies. Juno's placement and aspects tell you how you relate to other people, what is important to you in partnerships, and how you define your sense of belonging. Do you cherish drama or prefer the steady course? Juno tells you your partnership preferences, both what you want and what you expect from others.

The Tarot's Major Arcana card the Lovers represents Juno's ⚵ influence on partnerships and relationships.

Juno's natural affiliation with Water sign Scorpio ♏ facilitates intuition and emotion, with Air sign Libra ♎ bringing harmony and balance. Juno in your 6th or 10th house says you're drawn to jobs with a strong potential for staying. You might grow the better part of your career working for the same company, especially if your Juno is in earthy, committed Taurus ♉. Juno in Cancer ♋ suggests a more cautious, but ultimately dedicated, working relationship.

143

Pallas Athene ♀: Winner's Circle

The feminine counterpart of Mars ♂, the *yang* planet of action and boldness, *yin* Pallas Athene ♀ brings "warrior wisdom" to her placement in your birth chart. This goddess sprang from the head of her father, the god Jupiter, grown, armored, and ready for battle! She's all about winning, no question. But *how* you win matters as much as *that* you win, and fair competition is the only path to the winner's circle under this goddess's guide. But prestige and esteem are yours once you make the circle, as everyone admires and respects the winner of a fair competition.

Pallas Athene's natural affiliation with Fire sign Leo ♌ and Air signs Aquarius ♒ and Libra ♎ gives supportive Elemental energy to this asteroid's influences. The blend of Fixed and Cardinal qualities shows that "give up" is not in the vocabulary when Pallas Athene rules. When she's in your 6th house of work or your 10th house of career, you could be unstoppable. Pallas Athene's warrior orientation supports strategic planning in partnership with intuitive perception, tempering (critics might say masking!) aggression with sensitivity. Pallas Athene in Capricorn ♑ draws strength through accomplishment; in Sagittarius ♐ through adventure.

THE STAR.

The Tarot's Major Arcana card the Star represents the winning warrior asteroid, Pallas Athene ♀.

Vesta ⚶: Everything Is Everything

The Roman goddess of the hearth and the fourth of the asteroids that sky watchers discovered, Vesta's ⚶ is the brightest glow in the asteroid belt. When her orbit is just right—closest to the Sun and farthest from the Earth—you can see Vesta without a telescope. She shines her power of illumination wherever she resides in your birth chart, stripping away the shadows and bringing clarity to your focus. And that's what Vesta is all about—focus. She presses you to find and follow the single vision—not a goal or an objective along the way but on your destination and the journey that will carry you to it.

Her natural affiliations with Water Scorpio ♏ and Earth Virgo ♍ form a supportive Elemental foundation through which Vesta gives and expects loyalty and allegiance. Vesta in your 6th or 10th house can guide you to your ultimate success—fulfillment and self-actualization. As long as you stay on task (Virgo's influence), the flow goes with you (Scorpio's contribution). Slip off track, though, and you're likely to get bogged in the mud. Vesta in Aquarius ♒ seeks the path less traveled; Leo ♌ likes the route of companionship.

The Tarot's Major Arcana card the World represents the fulfillment and focus Vesta ⚶ brings.

Asteroid Influences: Katie Couric

Television journalist and co-host of the *Today* show for more than a decade, Katie Couric has interviewed some of the world's most influential—and camera-shy—newsmakers. She presents a combination of no-nonsense intelligence and compassionate sensitivity that encourages even the most reticent of her guests to open up. This is just what we might expect from someone with Ceres ⚳ in Aries ♈ in the 12th house of secrets. Let's look at the influence of the asteroids in Katie's birth chart. Arlene cast a birth chart using noon as Katie's birth time.

Katie's Ceres also is square her Sun ⚳ □ ☉, further bolstering the sense of connection that others feel with her. Even as a journalist seeking the truth people sometimes are reluctant to divulge, Katie conveys her nurturing qualities. She's tough but fair, and those sitting across from her know it. However, this is a challenging aspect. Katie has to work to let her nurturing tendencies come through in positive, supportive ways. On the flip side, she could be perceived as soft or callous.

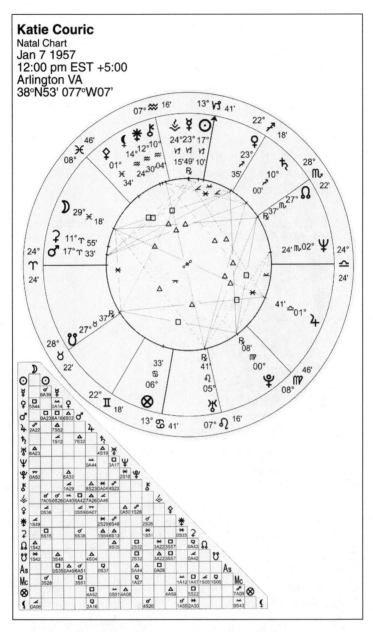

Katie Couric
Natal Chart
Jan 7 1957
12:00 pm EST +5:00
Arlington VA
38°N53' 077°W07'

*The goddess power of the asteroids provides strong support
for television journalist Katie Couric's career.*

Juno ⚸ and Pallas Athene ⚴ share residence in Katie's 11th house of humanitarianism and life purpose. Juno in Aquarius ♒ tells us she expects those in partnership with her to pull their own weight and to allow her the autonomy this fixed Air sign requires. When these expectations are met, Katie commits herself fully and unequivocally to the partnership. When they are not, things could get testy. Pallas Athene in Pisces ♓ affirms Katie's strength and courage through compassion, also giving a fighting edge to her determination that sometimes catches others by surprise.

Vesta ⚶ in Capricorn ♑ in Katie's 10th house of career indicates this is a woman who can indeed have it all. She is cautious yet generous, with Capricorn's Cardinal energy to drive her ambitions toward achievement. She is measured and organized—the grounding influence of this Earth sign. Vesta conjunct Mercury ⚶ ☌ ☿ says this woman communicates from a base of focus that is intent on stripping away whatever obscures the core. Vesta also is conjunct Katie's Sun ⚶ ☌ ☉, allowing Katie ease in expressing this inner dimension of herself.

Although the lack of a birth time meant Arlene had to cast a solar birth chart for Katie, it's very unlikely that this has any effect on the positions of the slow-moving asteroids.

Your Asteroids

How do the asteroids affect you? Each asteroid influences your perceptions and behaviors according to the sign of its placement. Here is a summary of keywords to help you identify each asteroid's influence in your birth chart.

Astro Sign of Asteroid's Placement	Ceres ⚳ You mentor through:	Juno ⚵ You partner through:	Pallas Athene ⚴ You find strength through:	Vesta ⚶ You reach fulfillment through:
Aries ♈	Enthusiasm	Impulse	Leadership	Competition
Taurus ♉	Stability	Commitment	Dependability	Solidarity
Gemini ♊	Reason	Informality	Versatility	Resourcefulness
Cancer ♋	Kindness	Devotion	Protection	Loyalty
Leo ♌	Generosity	Admiration	Creativity	Ingenuity
Virgo ♍	Benevolence	Practicality	Organization	Service
Libra ♎	Equity	Balance	Harmony	Integrity
Scorpio ♏	Ambition	Power	Transformation	Empowerment
Sagittarius ♐	Exploration	Excitement	Passion	Authenticity
Capricorn ♑	Caution	Reliability	Achievement	Credibility
Aquarius ♒	Innovation	Independence	Autonomy	Originality
Pisces ♓	Intuition	Idealism	Empathy	Compassion

Let's find the placement of the asteroids in your birth chart to see how they influence your work and career.

My Ceres ⚳ is in: _____
(Astro Sign)

So I mentor through: _____
(Keyword)

My Juno ⚵ is in: _____
(Astro Sign)

So I partner through: _____
(Keyword)

My Pallas Athene ⚴ is in: _____
(Astro Sign)

So I find strength through: _____
(Keyword)

My Vesta ⚶ is in: _____
(Astro Sign)

So I reach fulfillment through: _____
(Keyword)

Chiron ⚷, the Healer

Chiron was a god in the form of a centaur—upper body of a man, lower body of a horse. He had great wisdom and knowledge of healing, and taught his methods to the sons of the gods. During a lesson on poisons, Chiron accidentally pierced himself in the foot with a poison-tipped arrow. Chiron's immortality saved him from death but could not spare him from endless agony. Realizing his only relief was to pass from the earthly world, he gave up his immortality. Through death Chiron confronted, and consequently transcended, his suffering.

In Astrology, Chiron ⚷ represents the wounded healer. Chiron's placement in your birth chart might show where you have psychic or soul wounds—fears and worries you carry deep within you—that interfere with your ability to manifest your full potential, an influence that might show up in self-destructive behaviors. Instead of allowing yourself to succeed, you metaphorically shoot yourself in the foot. Katie Couric's Chiron is in Aquarius ♒ in her 11th house of humanitarianism and life goals, along with the asteroids Pallas Athene ⚴ and Juno ⚵, suggesting that her psychic healing may take place through her pursuit of her life's ambitions. Chiron's influence uncovers counterproductive patterns so you can confront them, understand them, correct them, and move on. What is the astrological sign and house placement of Chiron ⚷ in your birth chart?

My Chiron ⚷ is in _____ in my _____

                (Astro Sign)   (Astro House)

house of _____.

     (House Keyword)

Relationship Challenges

In Chapter 5 we introduced you to the synastry grid, Astrology's way of comparing the aspects of two charts to explore the strengths and challenges in relationships. There, we looked at a synastry grid for Bill Gates and Microsoft. We're going back to the synastry grid now, but to look at the working relationship between two people: actors Ben Affleck and Matt Damon, whose collaboration as college buddies rocketed them to the top of Hollywood's hit list—hit movie stars, that is. The pair wrote and played the starring roles in the film *Good Will Hunting*, which earned them an Academy Award for Best Original Screenplay in 1998.

First, let's look at the birth charts for these talented stars.

What a wonderful grand trine in Matt's chart! His expressive Capricorn ♑ Moon residing in his 12th house of secrets trines his Mercury (the planet of communication) and Pluto in his 8th house of transformation and his Mars in his 7th house of partnership ☽ △ ☿ ♀ ♂. And look at that full 8th house! Astrologers call this a stellium—three or more planets that are conjunct ☌ each other. A stellium creates an immense focus of the energy in areas the house of the stellium's location governs. Matt's stellium in his 8th house provides added focus for him to use the resources of others, as well as his own resources, wisely.

Want a guarantee of accomplishment? It doesn't get any better than this! Matt's Moon also trines his Saturn in his 3rd house of communication ☽ △ ♄, certainly a favorable aspect for a writer. Saturn also trines Matt's Pluto and Mars ♄ △ ♀ ♂, strong support for constructing his creative messages in ways that reach and connect with the general public.

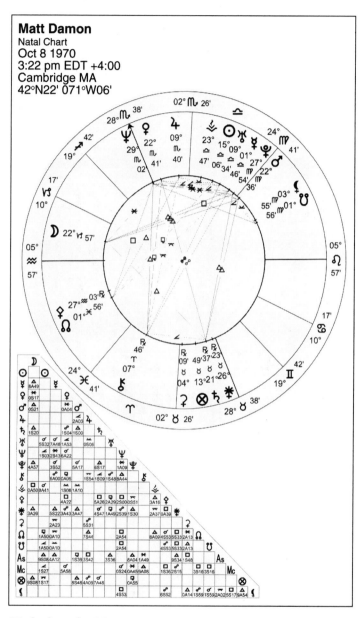

Birth chart for Matt Damon.

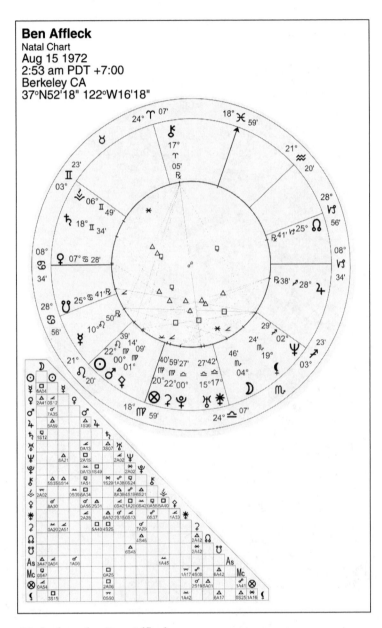

Ben Affleck
Natal Chart
Aug 15 1972
2:53 am PDT +7:00
Berkeley CA
37°N52'18" 122°W16'18"

Birth chart for Ben Affleck.

A pair of trines align Ben's Chiron ⚷ in Aries ♈ in the 10th house of career with his Leo ♌ Mercury ☿ in the 2nd house of values and money as well as with his Leo ♌ Sun ☉ in the 3rd house of communication. Whew! Another powerhouse lineup. The Sun in its natural sign of Leo supercharges this fiery, driving energy; with such configurations, Ben would *have* to express himself through writing. But just in case he might get a case of artistic self-doubt, there are Pallas Athene ⚴ and Mars ♂, both in organized Virgo ♍, to keep him on fire and on task!

What could possibly go wrong with such a partnership as Affleck and Damon's? Let's take a look at the synastry grid for these two for some insights into their (surprisingly many) challenges.

Across	Down
Matt Damon	**Ben Affleck**
Natal Chart	Natal Chart
Oct 8 1970	Aug 15 1972
3:22 pm EDT +4:00	2:53 am PDT +7:00
Cambridge, MA	Berkeley CA
42°N22' 071°W06'	37°N52'18" 122°W16'18"

	☽	☉	☿	♀	♂	♃	♄	♅	♆	♇	⚷	⚸	♀	✴	?	☊	☋	As	Mc	⊗	☽
☽							∠2A50	♂4A54	⚹3A00		7S44		∆0S37	♂2S50	✶2S50	□1A11					✶0S51
☉	π0A18			□0A01	⚸0S03		□1S03	∠1A55	□6A23		⚹0A07	✶1A07	⚸4A23	□3A44				♂9A17		□5A59	
☿							□1A10	✶1A16		∆3A04			□6A41				⚸4A53				□2S59
♀		□5S42	⚹0A13				∆2A12	∠0S51	□2A06		□0A18						∆5S31			π1S30	
♂		∠0S08	π1A32						□1S12		⚸3S11	□3S51	∆3A55	⚸1A42	♂1A42			□1S36			♂3A41
♃		□3S07		□6A02						π0S24	□0A45		✶1A36	π2A15	∆5S31		∆3S18		∆0A00	π0S10	∆5S17
♄	∆3S28			□4A02						∆9S00			∆5A13	♂8A28		∆0A35		π2A23			
♅	∆0S21								♂5S53	∠1S25			∆8A20			π1A29	π1A29	⚹9S30	∠1S49	π1S38	
♆			✶0S43						∠3S27	∆5A17	⚹5S27	♂6S06	∆1A40	□0S33	□0S33	∆3A28	∆3S51				□1A26
♇	∆7S30	♂1A18	♂7S51				∆8S51	♂9A07	∠1S25	∆2S34	♂7A19		∆4S04			π1A29	π1A29	∆5A30	✶1S49	□1S39	
⚷	□5S52	♂1A59						♂7A31			∆9A19	♂6S42				∠0A09	♂0A09				□1S50
⚸	□1A09	∆8A17	∆5S03					π2A51		∆2A45	∆8S55	✶0A57	□1A58			∆4S52	∆4S52	∆0S51			□2S53
♀	∠1S03	π0A37							□2S07		♂4S06	□4S46	∆3A00	♂0A47	♂0A47		□2S31				♂2A46
✴	□5A15	♂2S36							♂6A05	∆9A21					□0S46	∠0S46					∠1A13
?	∆0S02					♂8A47	✶0S18	♂0S22	∠1A41	∆1S22			♂4A55			π0A48	∆3A25				∆9S10
☊	♂2A44					∆6S05	✶3A01	∆3A05		∆4A04	∆2S13				□1A54	π1S21	∆0S42			✶2S57	
☋	♂2A44						∆3A01	✶3A05		∆3S21	π2S13				∆1A54	π1S21	∆0S42			∆2S57	
As	□6A32	□6A48	⚸0A53					∆1A06	∠1A57	□1A00	∆0A48					∠2A50	♂6A37			π2A36	
Mc	✶3A58						∆3A41	♂3A37	∆9A19	✶2A38	♂8A54				∠0A10			∆1A58	∆9A39		
⊗	∆2A17						✶2A00	♂1A56	∆0A57		♂7A13			∆5A43	∆1A31			□0A17			∆6A51
☽	✶3A33						♂3A17	✶3A12		♂2A13			♂9A38				♂6A59			♂9A14	♂5S35

In this synastry grid, Matt Damon is across and Ben Affleck is down.

The first thing we notice is the number of aspects these two share. Looking at the planets from the Moon ☽ through Ceres ⚳, here's what we find.

Astro Aspect	Influence	Number in Synastry Grid
Conjunction ☌	Intensifies energy of the aspected planets; can be supportive or challenging	15
Sextile ⚹	Favorable with focus on energies planets represent	7
Square ☐	Challenging but presents greatest opportunities and potential	20
Trine △	Harmonious, flowing, effortless	22
Quincunx ⚻	Challenging, need to make adjustments	5
Opposition ☍	Confrontational but presents opportunities if can work through challenges	9

Ben's Sun quincunx Matt's Moon ☉ ⚻ ☽ suggests these collaborators often need to adjust to each other's approaches to expression. Matt's Moon ☽ in Capricorn ♑ and its trine △ to Mercury ☿ puts a lot of emotion behind his words and actions, while Ben's Leo ♌ Sun ☉ just wants to get it said and done. Ben's Mercury squares his Moon ☿ ☐ ☽, telling us it's likely Matt who does most of the adjusting. This can create a sense of imbalance in their partnership, with Matt sometimes feeling everything has to be Ben's way or no way. Ben's Sun also squares Matt's Venus, Saturn, Neptune, and Juno ☉ ☐ ♀ ♄ ♆ ⚵, setting the stage for potential struggles regarding artistic control.

Those conjunct Plutos ♀ ☌ ♀ present the greatest risk for conflict. Conjunctions intensify the energies of the aspected planets, and Pluto is itself an intense influence. Pluto transforms and regenerates. There's no mistaking Pluto's power in initiating changes that alter the course of life for entire generations. Pluto energy is about as subtle as a forest fire, often leaving complete destruction in its wake. But from the ashes arise, Phoenix-like, new growth, opportunities, and structures. When personal Plutos are conjunct ☌, those who share this potent energy must take care to protect, not destroy, each other.

These are not insurmountable challenges—obviously, as their collaborations continue to earn them respect and honors. But each needs his space, too, which we see them accommodate by taking roles and functions independent of one another. Will these talented stars continue their creative collaborations? The abundance of favorable aspects—like those 22 trines—suggests that we will enjoy their endeavors for many years to come.

You can look for potential challenges in relationships by examining the synastry grid for yourself and your company or job in a similar way. Or if you have the birth information of a work colleague or a potential (or actual!) business partner, you can have an astrologer prepare birth charts and a synastry grid to look deeper into the nature of your collaboration.

Spin the Wheel of Fortune

We can't get you on the television show (sorry) but we can give you a spin on the Tarot's Wheel of Fortune, with a reading you can do for insight and perspective about your job decisions. This Major Arcana card represents change through factors that aren't always within your control. (Sound familiar?) First we show you an example reading, then we set you up to do a reading for yourself.

The Tarot's Wheel of Fortune symbolizes change and chance ... what some might call fate.

Cornelius has worked for his present company for seven years, advancing steadily through the ranks to his current position as lead technician. Over the past six months Wanda, his new manager, has been giving most of the complex troubleshooting projects to the three staff technicians, leaving Cornelius to handle the mundane assignments. He's talked with Wanda three times, most recently just last week when he asked her bluntly if she was preparing to eliminate his job. Not at all, she assured him. To the contrary, she wanted to promote him after the new fiscal year in three months.

But Monday Wanda asked Cornelius to start keeping a productivity journal, and he suspects this marks a fast track to unemployment. On Wednesday Cornelius got a phone call from a headhunter wanting Cornelius to interview for a job in Boston. The company seems to know a lot about him, and Cornelius is intrigued. He's worked hard to build his career where he is, but now he's not so sure the company wants him as much as he wants to stay. So he asks the cards, *"Should I meet with the headhunter?"*

The Tarot's Wheel of Fortune symbolizes change and chance, the unknowns in life. In numerology, the number of this card, 10, symbolizes completion and rebirth—the end of one cycle and the start of the next. This spread starts by pulling the Wheel of Fortune card from the deck and placing it in the center—the hub.

Cornelius then focuses on his question and shuffles the remaining cards. When he feels ready, he begins to place them in position. The first four cards go *face down* around the wheel clockwise, starting with the "T" and moving to the "A," "R," and "O" positions along the wheel. Remember, these cards go face down! They represent the factors that are beyond your control; these are the cards of chance.

Next, place four cards *face up* on top of the cards around the wheel, again starting with "T" and moving clockwise. These are the cards of change, and they represent the factors that are within your ability to influence if you choose. The tenth and final card goes *face down* over the Wheel of Fortune card. It represents the "wild card" spin of fate. Where will the wheel stop? Nobody knows!

The face-up cards tell the story of the events Cornelius can influence, although these are cards of impending change. There are no surprises here, just affirmation of what Cornelius suspects.

4 of Pentacles. At the "T" at the top of the wheel, this card tells Cornelius he's holding on to his assets—literally. With his manager giving his work away, Cornelius struggles to keep a grip on his job.

4 of Wands R. At the "A" position on the wheel of chance, more evidence of change. Is the party over for Cornelius? It sure looks like it!

3 of Wands R. At the "R" position, another reversed card. Once again, things are falling away, including the very tools of trade. Cornelius's work goes to other people and his skills suffer. Perhaps the situation is even worse than he suspected; if that golden sea is his company, Cornelius's ships are falling out of the water.

5 of Swords. Well, well, what have we here at the "O" position? Could it be Wanda, conniving to send Cornelius on his way? The sneaky guy has all the swords, the two walking away have lost theirs. Are those storm clouds moving in?

The face-up cards are the cards of impending change when you spin Tarot's Wheel of Fortune.

The next four cards around the circle tell the story of the events that are beyond Cornelius's ability to control or change. They provide insights into whether the previous four cards represent a worthwhile fight for Cornelius, and some hints about what might be ahead for his career. Cornelius now turns the cards around the wheel's perimeter face up.

The next four cards show the factors that are beyond control or influence.

Queen of Swords. The top of the wheel at the "T" position is where the wheel starts. Is this the headhunter who wants to interview Cornelius for the job in Boston? We think so, and Cornelius agrees. And it looks to us like she's already made up her mind to offer that job to him!

6 of Cups. At the "A" position, what a lovely card of joy and nostalgia. When Cornelius looks at this card he thinks of his friend from college, Chloe. They started working in the same department, then Chloe moved to the East Coast somewhere. Say, you don't suppose ...?

2 of Wands. At the "R" position, this character watches and waits. For his ship to come sailing into port? Could be. He's worked hard to get to where he is, and now he has the world in the palm of his hand—literally. Cornelius immediately identifies with this image, feeling it represents him where he is in his career.

4 of Swords R. At first this card at the "O" position frightens Cornelius. Is he going to die? Arlene assures him this card means exactly the opposite—it's time for him to get up and get going! The 4 of Swords reversed signals the end of a difficult time and the start of new opportunities. It's an action card, full of *yang* energy, so the path might be tumultuous at times.

And now it's time for the final card, the card that represents what the Wheel of Fortune holds for Cornelius. Will he lose a turn or advance to the next round? Let's turn over the card and see!

The center card represents the "wild card" of fate, the random spin of the Wheel of Fortune.

Temperance. What a spin! Have patience, Cornelius. Work with the people who want to help you, and abundance is yours. We suggest you waste no time calling that headhunter ...

The cards Cornelius drew gave a clear and unmistakable answer. Had Cornelius remained uncertain of the information, we would look also at the relationships between the pairs of cards for additional clues and insights.

Now you try it! Here is the spread form and the steps to do your own reading.

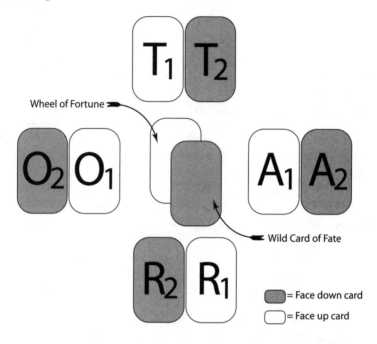

Wheel of Fortune

Wild Card of Fate

= Face down card

= Face up card

1. Formulate your question. Be as specific as you can. Write it here:

   _____

2. Put the Wheel of Fortune card in the center, face up.
3. Focus on your question and shuffle the rest of your Tarot deck.
4. Lay out the next four cards *face down* at the T-A-R-O of the wheel, starting with "T" and moving clockwise. These are the cards of chance; you cannot influence their outcome although you can choose a course of action to accommodate the changes they reflect.
5. Lay out the next four cards *face up* over the first layer. These are the cards of change; although they represent circumstances that will change, you can influence them.
6. Place the final card face down over the Wheel of Fortune card in the center. This card represents the spin of the wheel, the "wild card" of fate and the ultimate outcome.

Starting with the card in the "T" position at the top of the wheel, look at each card. What does it tell you about your question and your situation? Spend plenty of time with the card, so you get all of the information it can provide for you. Do this for each of the face-up cards along the wheel. Write the cards and your perceptions here:

T-1 Card: _____

Perceptions: _____

A-1 Card: _____

Perceptions: _____

R-1 Card: _____

Perceptions: _____

O-1 Card: _____

Perceptions: _____

When you're ready, turn over the face-down cards around the wheel's perimeter. (Leave the center card face down.) Place them beside or over the first layer of cards. Look at each one in order, as you did with the first layer. Write the cards and your perceptions here:

T-2 Card: _____

Perceptions: _____

A-2 Card: _____

Perceptions: _____

R-2 Card: _____

Perceptions: _____

O-2 Card: _____

Perceptions: _____

Does the information the cards present make sense to you? And how about your "wild card" outcome? What fate do you divine in your Wheel of Fortune Spread?

Wild Card: _____

Perceptions: _____

If the answer to your question still seems unclear, look at the pairs of cards together to understand how they relate to each other and gain deeper insight.

chapter 8

A Lifework for Eternity

Exploring the karmic messages of your birth chart's Nodes
Present you, meet past you: Psychic Intuition time travel
The lessons of Tarot's Karmic Spread
Saturn's touchpoints
Uncovering Saturn's lessons in your life
Goals, ideals, and your 11th house
Past, present, and future: Tarot tells the story of your mission

Arlene talks a lot with her clients about finding their "bliss" in work and career. This is a much bigger picture than simply finding a job that you like. It often becomes the driving force behind restlessness and the urge to move on. Your soul has knowledge to impart and lessons to learn! You're not looking for just a job: You're looking for the career of your life, the lifework that can carry you through the days as well as support your soul's evolution. By now, you've used the tools of the Intuitive Arts—Astrology, Tarot, and Psychic Intuition—in a number of ways to deepen your understanding of your talents, abilities, tendencies, needs, and challenges. In this chapter, we explore ways to apply your insights for fulfillment, and as Maslow would say, "self-actualization," in your quest for work that nourishes your soul.

Nodes of Knowledge

Astrology identifies two karmic points in your birth chart, the North Node ☊ and the South Node ☋, which represent the lessons you need to learn and the learning you've brought into this life with you. They are always directly opposite each other in your chart, as they were in the sky at the moment of your birth. The nodes mark the two points at which the orbit of the Moon ☽ around the Earth intersects the orbit of the Earth around the Sun ☉—the North Node as the Moon's orbit moves from north to south, and the South Node as the Moon's orbit moves from south to north.

Like other influences in your birth chart, each Node belongs to the sign of the Zodiac that it's in at the time of your birth, and resides within the corresponding house. Your South Node ☋ is your comfort zone. It represents what you've already learned about how to get along in the world—your methods of communicating, forming relationships, and so on. Some of these methods support your efforts to grow and advance, although many are the counterproductive habits that keep you trapped where you are. When you want to know why you're in the same kind of dead-end job *again,* astrologers like Arlene will turn to your South Node ☋ for answers and insights.

Your North Node ☊ represents what you need to learn in this lifetime for your soul to evolve. "Great! Lead on!" you might think. After all, this is the direction of opportunity, right? Indeed. But it's also the direction of change. And for as much as we all *say* we want to grow and advance, we resist *doing* anything to change. Change is challenge, and challenge is uncomfortable if not, sometimes, downright painful.

Your North Node ☊ won't indulge your resistance. If anything, it will pull you and tug you in the direction you need to move. When you want to know where you're headed, if you're on the right path, your North Node holds the answers. The astrological signs and house placements of your Nodes tell you how you will move from South to North in this lifetime, for your soul's fulfillment. The aspect with the most significant influence is a conjunction ☌, where 10° or less separate the planet and the Node—they're literally side by side. Conjunctions intensify the aspected planet's energy.

When we look at the birth chart for talented actor Robert Downey Jr., we see that his North Node ☊ is in Gemini ♊ in his 11th house of humanitarianism and his South Node ☋ is in Sagittarius ♐ in his 5th house of creativity. We can see Robert's foundation of self-expression under the archer's targeted enthusiasm—the influence of his South Node ☋—play out in the success of his career. His North Node ☊ placement tells us that Robert's lessons in this lifetime require him to move from self-focus to working for the betterment of society at large. Robert gets a boost from some supportive aspects as he works to make that shift, with his North Node sextile his ascendant as well as his Sun and his Venus ☊ ⚹ ☉ ♀. A harmonious trine Pallas Athene ☊ △ ⚴ in his 6th house of career encourages him to use his talents for personal progress. But there are some challenging aspects, too, with squares to five planets: Mars, Saturn, Uranus, Pluto, and Chiron ☊ □ ♂ ♄ ♅ ♇ ⚷. There is great opportunity for Robert to transform the world through his artistry, but it will take considerable effort, dedication, and focus.

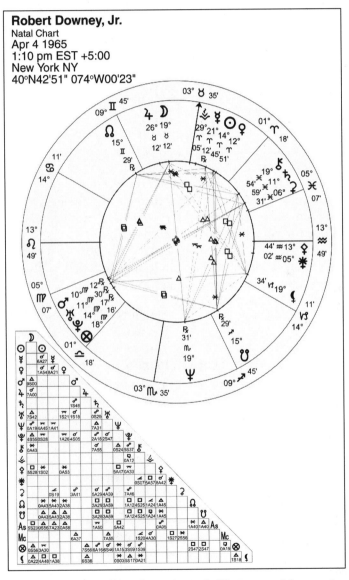

Robert Downey, Jr.
Natal Chart
Apr 4 1965
1:10 pm EST +5:00
New York NY
40°N42'51" 074°W00'23"

The North Node ☊ and South Node ☋ signs and houses in actor Robert Downey Jr.'s birth chart.

Robert's South Node ☋ provides challenges similar to those in his North Node ☊, suggesting there is an intense legacy of counterproductive behaviors that want to keep him in their grip. There's the same lineup of squared aspects: ☋ □ ♂ ♄ ♅ ♀ ⚷. We often see challenging aspects to Chiron, the wounded healer, when people struggle with addictive and self-destructive behaviors like those that have plagued Robert's career and life from time to time. It's a little easier for him to follow these patterns, with his South Node ☋ trine △ his ascendant; this is a more effortless flow than the North Node ☊ sextile ✳ ascendant aspect.

Nodal Concepts

We gave you a comprehensive look at Robert Downey Jr.'s Nodes so you can see how much information Nodes can provide when it comes to looking at your career as a vehicle that carries you toward your soul's mission. To get you started on an exploration of the messages in your own Nodes, we've created two tables that identify the primary characteristics of each placement—one for your Nodes and their astrological signs and one for your Nodes and their houses.

This first table shows the Nodes and the keywords for their astrological signs. The signs identify your soul lessons and the foundation of knowledge or abilities that you will use to learn them.

North Node ☊ in Astro Sign	South Node ☋ in Astro Sign	North Node ☊ Keyword *You need to learn:*	South Node ☋ Keyword *From a foundation of:*
Aries ♈	Libra ♎	Leadership	Collaboration
Taurus ♉	Scorpio ♏	Self-sufficiency	Value
Gemini ♊	Sagittarius ♐	Communication	Integrity
Cancer ♋	Capricorn ♑	Mentoring	Dedication
Leo ♌	Aquarius ♒	Passion	Innovation
Virgo ♍	Pisces ♓	Productivity	Compassion
Libra ♎	Aries ♈	Partnership	Ingenuity
Scorpio ♏	Taurus ♉	Authority	Ownership
Sagittarius ♐	Gemini ♊	Authenticity	Intellect
Capricorn ♑	Cancer ♋	Responsibility	Protectiveness
Aquarius ♒	Leo ♌	Generosity	Enthusiasm
Pisces ♓	Virgo ♍	Sensitivity	Efficiency

This second table shows the Nodes and the key phrases for their house placements. The houses tell where and how you will use your foundation to learn and build toward the future.

North Node ☊ in Astro House	South Node ☋ in Astro House	North Node ☊ Key Phrase *What you need to do to grow:*	South Node ☋ Key Phrase *What's comfortable for you:*
1st house *self*	7th house *partnership*	Take the initiative	Letting others make the decisions
2nd house *values*	8th house *transformation*	Develop beliefs that are personal to you	The status quo
3rd house *communication*	9th house *philosophy*	Do the research	Winging it
4th house *home*	10th house *career*	Cultivate personal and family relationships	A life centered around work
5th house *creativity*	11th house *humanitarianism*	Develop and work toward long-term goals	Taking what comes and moving on when it's done
6th house *work*	12th house *secrets*	Play by the common rules	Living in your own world
7th house *partnership*	1st house *self*	Trust others	Making your own way
8th house *transformation*	2nd house *values*	Accept differing views	Your personal value system
9th house *philosophy*	3rd house *communication*	Express your own thoughts	Playing the sounding board
10th house *career*	4th house *home*	Establish a career path	Job-hopping
11th house *humanitarianism*	5th house *creativity*	Mentor others	Being in the spotlight
12th house *secrets*	6th house *work*	Share your expertise by teaching what you know to others	Stepping in whenever someone needs a helping hand

From these pairings, you can begin to glean insights about why you think and behave in certain ways and consider whether those approaches are supportive or challenging for you.

Identify the Karmic Messages Your Nodes Carry

Now let's let you apply this information to you. Do you have your birth chart? Locate the sign and house placements of your North Node ☊ and your South Node ☋ and write them here:

North Node ☊ Sign: _____

South Node ☋ Sign: _____

North Node ☊ House: _____

South Node ☋ House: _____

Now, go to the table for the astrological signs of the Nodes and find the keywords that apply to your Node combination. Circle them. Next, go to the table for the houses of the Nodes and find the key phrases that apply to your Node combination. Circle them. Got them? Good! Use them to complete your birth chart's karmic summary.

We've filled one in for Robert Downey Jr. to give you an example. Looking back at his birth chart, we remind ourselves that his North Node ☊ is in Gemini ♊ in the 11th house and his South Node ☋ is in Sagittarius ♐ in the 5th house. So here's the karmic message Robert's Nodes have for him:

Functioning from a foundation of **integrity**, Robert is comfortable **being in the spotlight**. He will grow toward fulfilling his soul's purpose when he learns to use **communication** to **mentor others**.

See where we got everything? Take a moment to make sure; track the bolded words back to the tables we drew them from. Now, do the same for your information to create your personal karmic summary.

Functioning from a foundation of _____, I am comfortable _____. I will grow toward fulfilling my soul's purpose when I learn to use _____ to _____.

Don't panic if you can't see your way from your South Node ☋ to your North Node ☊! It's your *lifetime* mission to fulfill your soul's bliss. No one can do it all at once. But you—yes, even you!—can make sure, steady progress. Select one function or behavior to change this month. Practice and work toward that change every day. By the end of the month, it will be a change no longer, but simply the way you do things! Write your first change here, so you can get started:

This month I will do _____ instead of

(new function or behavior)

_____.

(old function or behavior)

This will help me learn to use _____ to

(Ω keyword)

to _____.

(Ω key phrase)

Somewhere (Else) in Time

Let's exercise your Psychic Intuition. Choose another time in history— any time, any place. Pick a past life, if you like. What would your job look like in that time and place? How would you dress for work, where would you go to work, and what would your workplace look like? What would be the tools of your trade? Would you have a job similar to the one you now have, or would you work in a different career? What would be the course of your workday?

Write a synopsis of this other life, past or imaginary, here:

_____

_____

Now sit in a relaxed position and let your Psychic Intuition take over. Using your mind's eye, your psychic Third Eye, envision yourself going through the day. *Become* yourself in this other life. Feel the fabric of the clothing you're wearing. Is it coarse or soft, does it make noise when you walk or sit? What do you hold in your hands right now? What are you doing? Are there other people around? What skills do you possess? How do you apply them, and how do you receive recognition for your abilities? Do you feel appreciated?

Now envision the you of the present approaching this you in the past. How can he or she enlighten and assist you in your present work?

What questions would you ask? Ask them! What answers do you get? At last, you can ask anything you like without worry or fear. There's no competition or jealousy, just the present you talking with a past you. What advice can you give yourself? What does this person of the past know that can help you now? Indulge the experience of this past life for 10 minutes, and then write your perceptions:

See if you can find an "artifact" that represents your job or career in this life of the past. Look around in flea markets and antique shops. It doesn't have to be anything elaborate or expensive. Are you a teacher in this other life? Look for an old textbook, slate and chalk, or even a "stylus" you fashion from a stick for doing figures or glyphs in the dirt. Are you a healer, a doctor or a nurse? You might find an old surgical tool or medicine bottle, or some medicinal herbs.

Put the item in your workspace or office, if you can. Whenever you want a consultation with this past you, hold or look at the artifact and let it serve as your psychic connection.

Karmic Messages

When Marietta, Charissa's boss, greeted Charissa with, "I need this report for the strategy meeting at 10 this morning. Steve's out sick and you're the only one who knows the format," it was an all-too-familiar refrain. After two years, she still wasn't doing the work she'd hired on to do. She was supposed to be out in the field, doing on-site consultations with clients. Instead, she spent her time doing what amounted to odd jobs and clerical assignments.

Charissa was confused and frustrated. She'd gone back to school to improve her skills and break out of this pattern, yet here she was, right back in it. Arlene suggested a Tarot Karmic Spread, which would help Charissa identify her current karmic lessons—those persistent lessons we repeat again and again until we finally master them.

The Karmic Spread is one of the rare Tarot readings for which everyone asks the same question: "What karmic lessons am I learning now?" Just four cards give a surprising amount of information. Charissa shuffled the Tarot deck and when she felt ready, she placed four cards in the Karmic Spread.

Charissa's four-card Karmic Spread gave her Justice, the Sun R, King of Cups, and 3 of Swords R.

Right away we notice two of Charissa's cards are Major Arcana, which are the Tarot's karmic cards. They address lessons that might span a lifetime (or more!) and touch many facets of your life. You can influence the circumstances that will lead you along their paths, but you cannot change the events that Major Arcana cards represent.

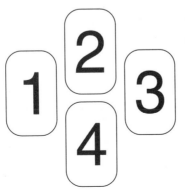

The Tarot's Karmic Spread.

Now it's your turn. *"What karmic lessons am I learning now?"* What do the cards tell you about your current karmic lessons?

Although the question for the Karmic Spread remains constant— "What karmic lessons am I learning now?"—the answer will change as you move to different lessons. When you receive cards that don't make sense to you even after you meditate on their possible meanings, do a second reading. This time, tell the cards: "I don't quite understand. Please show me more about the karmic lessons I'm learning now."

Saturn's Lessons

Saturn ♄, the planetary teacher and taskmaster, returns to its natal position in your birth chart about every 29 years. This planet has a somewhat irregular orbit, taking between 28½ and 29½ years to make its way through the Zodiac. When Saturn conjuncts itself ♄ ♂ ♄ in your birth chart, as we talked about in Chapter 7, its pressure is unmistakable. This is your Saturn return, when Saturn's position in the Zodiac returns to its placement at your birth. You find yourself taking stock of your life, particularly your work and career. Saturn ♄ wants you to focus clearly and purposefully on what you're doing and why—and if you're off-track, to correct yourself.

Saturn's travel through the Zodiac hits other touchpoints in your life, too. These are Saturn's quarter-points, when Saturn is square or in opposition to itself ♄ □ ♄ or ♄ ♂ ♄. During these aspects, your work efforts might seem to stall. Things take longer than they should and workloads intensify. You feel this nudging (which sometimes has all the subtlety of a shove in the back) from Saturn about every 7½ years.

What's with this celestial persistence, anyway? You'd think returning every 30 years to jolt us back on track would be enough! As the myth goes, Saturn is a composite of the ancient Roman god of the same name who ruled the harvest and of the Greek god Cronus, the god of time. Order and productivity being the essence of his nature, he taught the Romans the timing of agriculture—when to plow and sow, how to cultivate and nurture the growing crops, and when to harvest. Year in and year out, it's the cycle of the planting that generates sustenance.

So it is with your career. You plow, you sow, you cultivate, you harvest—as much as what's growing takes off on its own, it still requires your constant attention. It is the cycle of career as it is the cycle of life. However grand your visions, manifesting them as reality still takes place one step at a time. Saturn comes around to make sure you're taking those steps, and that they're carrying you in the right direction.

Saturn, like any good teacher, only wants for you to become who and what you are capable of—which is what you want, too, isn't it? Saturn wants you to reach your fulfillment, to find your bliss as you leave your mark in this world. Put in other terms, Saturn pushes you to attain the pinnacle of Maslow's pyramid: self-actualization. We can see Saturn's influence on this cycle with amazing clarity in Bruce Springsteen's birth chart. In Chapter 2 we looked at how Bruce's natal Sun ☉ shapes his career; here we'll bring back his chart to take a look at the guidance of his natal Saturn ♄.

Bruce's natal Saturn ♄ is in Virgo ♍ in his 4th house of home, telling us the family structure is important to Bruce and he's willing to put forth the effort necessary to develop and maintain a supportive home environment. At his first brush with Saturn's influence, around age 7, Bruce credits seeing Elvis Presley perform on the *Ed Sullivan Show* with igniting his interest in being a musician. This was the first time Saturn squared itself ♄ □ ♄ in Bruce's birth chart.

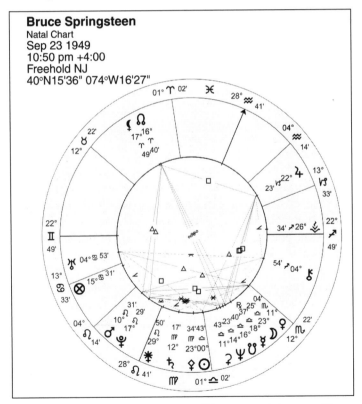

Bruce's natal Saturn ♄ is in Virgo ♍ in his 4th house of home.

When Saturn moved into opposition with itself ♄ ☍ ♄ 7 years later, at age 14, Bruce bought his first guitar. At age 23 he signed his first recording contract—Saturn's second squaring in his birth chart. And by the time he was 30, the time of his Saturn ♄ return, Bruce was well on his way to becoming a legend in rock 'n' roll. Music critics consider the album he recorded around that time—*Nebraska*—his first that showed his maturity as a musician. Saturn must've been pleased!

Saturn's residence in Bruce's 4th house of home is a clear clue that not all is work-related for this hardworking man. As it seems Bruce didn't act on this part of Saturn's message during his Saturn return, Saturn brought it back to him with its next square. At age 36, Bruce married Julianne Phillips. It was a relationship that challenged them both from the beginning, however, in part because of the demands of Bruce's career, and within a few years it ended in divorce. When Arlene runs a transit chart for Bruce's 36th birthday to look for Saturn's position at this time, she finds Saturn ♄ transiting Scorpio ♏ in his 6th house of work. No surprise there!

By the time of his next Saturn opposition ♄ ☍ ♄, Bruce was married again—to a singer in his band—and a father. These Saturn touchpoints were not easy for him, but through his work—music that resonates the power of his lessons in ways that we can connect with as we confront our own Saturn pressures—he met his challenges head-on and turned them into opportunities.

Learning Saturn's Lessons

Like the karmic messages of your North and South Nodes, the lessons Saturn ♄ has for you depend on its sign and placement in your birth chart. There are two dimensions to this: the lesson you need to learn and the way that you will learn it. These, too, are lessons that span a lifetime. To help you begin exploring your Saturn influences, we've created two tables to identify the key traits of the sign and the house affiliation.

As Saturn ♄ teaches the lessons of karma, astrologers often consider its sign in your birth chart to be your karma sign. This first table shows Saturn's placement in each of the 12 Zodiac signs, which identifies the lesson Saturn has for you to learn.

When Your Saturn ♄ Is in the Astro Sign	Your Saturn ♄ Lesson Is	You Learn Your Saturn ♄ Lesson Through
Aries ♈	Patience	Following things through to completion
Taurus ♉	Self-worth	Measuring value in non-material ways
Gemini ♊	Commitment	Making decisions rather than letting things happen
Cancer ♋	Emotional balance	Looking at the facts rather than the feelings of situations
Leo ♌	Humility	Letting others take the spotlight
Virgo ♍	Open-mindedness	Seeing the bigger picture
Libra ♎	Independence	Trusting your own ability to make decisions and choices
Scorpio ♏	Trust	Being open and direct with others
Sagittarius ♐	Responsibility	Keeping promises
Capricorn ♑	Acceptance	Allowing mistakes to be lessons
Aquarius ♒	Cooperation	Working with others as a team
Pisces ♓	Structure	Organizing and planning activities and work efforts

This second table shows Saturn's placement in each of the 12 houses of the chart wheel and how that placement influences the ways in which you'll learn your Saturn lessons.

When Your Saturn ♄ Is in the Astro House	You Feel or Act	Your Path of Learning Is Your Ability To
1st house of self	Accountable to the demands of others	Assert your needs and desires
2nd house of values	Unsure of the value of your work	Earn income and invest wisely
3rd house of communication	Quiet and reserved	Express yourself and listen to others

When Your Saturn ♄ Is in the Astro House	You Feel or Act	Your Path of Learning Is Your Ability To
4th house of home	Like caring for others is a responsibility or burden	Nurture from a base of joy
5th house of creativity	Structured and task-oriented	Indulge spontaneity
6th house of work	Your work is your life	Enjoy recreational activities that have no connection to your work
7th house of partnership	Autonomous	Connect with others
8th house of transformation	Attached to the past	Accept and manage change
9th house of philosophy	Narrowly focused in your views	Open your mind to new ideas
10th house of career	Responsible for the efforts and progress of others	Delegate and share
11th house of humanitarianism	Alone, taking care of yourself	Socialize and take part in group activities
12th house of secrets	Overwhelmed and withdrawn	Accept help from others to gain insight and understanding

Saturn in Your Birth Chart

Where is Saturn ♄ in your birth chart? Locate the symbol, its sign, and its house and write the information here:

In my birth chart, Saturn ♄ is in the sign of _____ in the _____ house.

Now, go to the tables for Saturn's lessons. In the first table, find the sign your Saturn is in and write the corresponding lesson and way of learning it:

My Saturn ♄ lesson is _____ and I will learn this lesson through _____.

Then go to the second table of houses. Locate the house of Saturn's placement in your birth chart and write the corresponding influence and path of learning:

Saturn ♄ influences me to feel or act _____. My path of learning to meet this challenge and turn it into opportunity is to

_____.

We use Bruce Springsteen as an example so you can see how this works:

Bruce's Saturn ♄ is in the sign of **Virgo** ♍ in the **4th** house.

His Saturn ♄ lesson is **open-mindedness** and he will learn this lesson through **seeing the bigger picture.**

Saturn ♄ influences him to feel or act **like caring for others is a responsibility or burden.** His path of learning to meet this challenge and turn it into opportunity is to **nurture from a base of joy.**

The karmic messages of your Nodes ☊ ☋ and the karmic lessons of Saturn ♄ go together. Your Nodes carry the themes that guide your passage in life. Saturn adds the practical framework to help you follow those themes. They support and complete each other. It is the balance of existence.

Ideals of the 11th House

The 11th house of humanitarianism reflects your life's goals and ideals. This is where you become defined beyond your individuality for the contributions you can make on a larger scale to the community and to the world. This is where and how you put your talents to good use for the common good, and in so doing achieve your individual potential. Saturn ♄ and Uranus ♅ share rulership of the 11th house—an interesting balance of discipline and rebellion! The planets and signs in your 11th house define your approaches to your ideals and your sense of servitude for the betterment of society.

Author J. K. Rowling appears to have catapulted to success, fame, and fortune when the first of her Harry Potter books debuted as a mega-best-seller in 1997. Not so, she's quick to point out—she wrote her first book 20-some years earlier, around age 7—the time of her first Saturn square ♄ □ ♄! When we look at the stellium (three or more planets that are conjunct each other, a very potent alignment) in her 11th house, it's clear that through her communication skills, this woman will change the world. And indeed, she has.

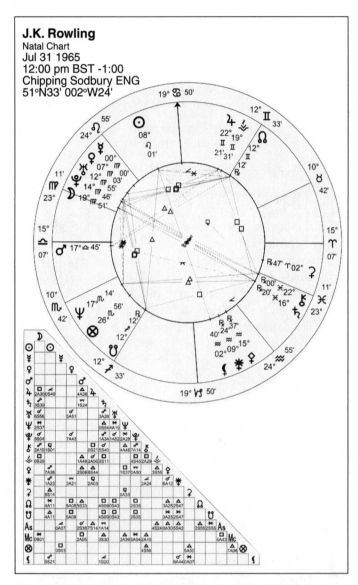

J.K. Rowling
Natal Chart
Jul 31 1965
12:00 pm BST -1:00
Chipping Sodbury ENG
51°N33' 002°W24'

*The stellium in author J. K. Rowling's Solar 11th house
presents a very potent alignment of planetary influences.*

Leo ♌, the sign of strength and fire, rules J. K.'s solar 11th house,
putting the power of confidence and persistence behind her efforts to
succeed in manifesting her ideals. First, let's take a closer look at that
phenomenal stellium, which includes:

Planet	Rules
Mercury ☿	Communication
Venus ♀	Money and beauty (art)
Uranus ♅	Originality and independence
Pluto ♇	Regeneration
Moon ☽	Intuition and emotion

All are in Earth sign Virgo ♍, the sign of service, sacred patterns, and diligence—and the planet of communication, Mercury ☿, rules. Uranus ♅ resides in its natural house, strengthening its already intense influence. How a birth chart could be more supportive of the goals of someone who wanted to write books from the time she could barely read them, we don't know! But look across the chart wheel at J. K.'s 5th house of creativity, where the insistent cosmic teacher, Saturn ♄, resides in Pisces ♓ and forms numerous aspects to the stellium in the 11th house as well as to planets throughout her birth chart. We count two oppositions, three squares, two trines, and one quincunx:

opposition Uranus, Moon, and Pluto ♄ ☍ ♅ ☽ ♇

square Vesta, North Node, and South Node ♄ □ ⚶ ☊ ☋

trine Neptune ♄ △ ♆ and midheaven

conjunct Chiron ♄ ☌ ⚷

quincunx ⚻ ascendant

These aspects tell us that success won't come easy for J. K., but if she can prevail through the challenges and hardships it will exceed her wildest dreams. In the five years she took to write *Harry Potter and the Philosopher's Stone* (published in the United States as *Harry Potter and the Sorcerer's Stone*), J. K. moved to Portugal to teach English, married, gave birth to a daughter, divorced, and moved back to her native England to again become a teacher—writing all the while in her "spare" time. When it was published, the fantasy story she wrote of a young wizard's path to his destiny became itself a publishing fantasy come true, breaking sales records and earning numerous awards. Neptune ♆ (planet of ideals and illusion) trine △ midheaven (manifestation of career), anyone?

What is the sign of your 11th house? How does it influence your goals and ideals? What planets are in your 11th house, and what aspects do they form? (Don't worry if there are no planets in your 11th house; not all houses contain planets.) You can look in Appendix A to refresh your memory of the keywords and key phrases that apply to your sign and planets.

11th house sign: _____

Key influences: _____

11th house planets: _____

Key influences: _____

11th house aspects: _____

Consider how these energies apply to your job and career. Do they support or challenge your efforts to move toward your ideals and goals? What can you do to make the most of them?

Tarot Tells the Story of Your Mission

What *is* your mission in this life? Are you certain about it, like Bruce Springsteen and J. K. Rowling? Or do you wonder as you wander through your life and perhaps from job to job or career to career? Whether you think you know or you really haven't a clue, Tarot's Mission Spread gives you some insights. This 21-card spread looks at your past, present, and future to tell a story about your purpose and path.

The first seven cards of the Mission Spread tell about your past—the path you've followed so far and where it's brought you. The second seven cards tell about your present—what's happening in your life and career, and what challenges are confronting you. The third seven cards tell you about your future—where your path is taking you and how you will move toward fulfillment. As the story unfolds, you'll be able to see where your gifts and talents are and how you can use them to learn your karmic lessons and advance in your life.

As you shuffle your cards, focus your thoughts on your sense of mission. For this reading, you don't need to ask a specific question; most of us have a swirl of questions when it comes to life purpose. The cards present a panorama for you to explore and contemplate. When you are ready to lay out your cards, put them in three rows of seven cards each.

Life's past mission and purpose

Life's present mission and purpose

Life's future mission and purpose

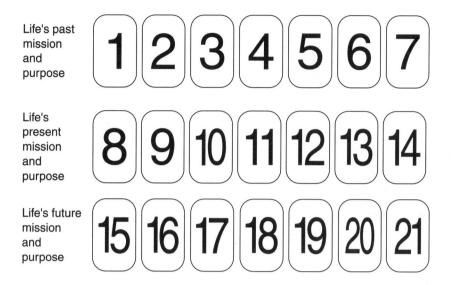

Here's how to lay out your cards for a Tarot Mission Spread.

Write down the cards you draw and your initial responses, so you can go back to them for further insights and study. Make sure you note whether a card is reversed; this alters the card's meaning to suggest delays, reconsiderations, challenges, or new directions. Look at each card individually and in sequence, and then look at the cards in relationship to one another. Does the "story" seem to flow in logical order?

Take note of how many cards are Major Arcana; these are cards of destiny. The outcomes they represent are beyond your ability to influence, although you can shape your actions and prepare your reactions to the events they might symbolize. The energies of these events are already in motion. Major Arcana cards often represent people in your workplace or life that have the ability to control or influence your job situation and career path. Notice, too, whether a particular suit of the Minor Arcana dominates any of the three rows or the spread overall. Explore all facets of meaning for the Minor Arcana cards, including timing.

Are there cards that don't make sense to you, or that seem out of place? If there are, note your reaction in your comments. It might make sense when you come back to it later—which could be a few weeks to several years from now. If there's one absolute Arlene has learned in her 20 years of reading Tarot, it's that the cards never lie. They don't always make sense, right away, but they always tell the story of what is about to be revealed.

These Major Arcana cards among your first seven cards might be telling you you have reached the point where you can let go of the past so you can move on to the future (Death), that now may be the time to focus your energy inward (the Hermit) to gain insight. Perhaps your fears (the Devil) have kept you from realizing your potential.

Your Mission Spread: The Past

This is the first row of cards that you lay down. It tells the story of the past as it relates to your mission or purpose in life and your path either toward or away from that purpose.

Card 1: _____

Response: _____

Card 2: _____

Response: _____

Card 3: _____

Response: _____

Card 4: _____

Response: _____

Card 5: _____

Response: _____

Card 6: _____

Response: _____

Card 7: _____

Response: _____

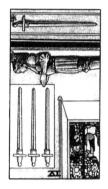  

These cards among your second seven cards might suggest that it's been a long haul but you're finally rested and ready to move on (4 of Swords R), you're cultivating the work that will take you to your future (7 of Pentacles), but there are still some lessons you need to learn and you're not quite firmly on your path yet (World R).

Your Mission Spread: The Present

This is the second row of cards that you lay down. It tells the story of what is happening right now—what decisions and challenges confront you, which people are supportive and who are trying to block your way, what hidden agendas might be lurking. Like the cards representing the past, these cards of the present show whether you are on track for your life's mission or if you've taken a detour.

Card 8: _____

Response: _____

Card 9: _____

Response: _____

Card 10: _____

Response: _____

Card 11: _____

Response: _____

Card 12: _____

Response: _____

Card 13: _____

Response: _____

Card 14: _____

Response: _____

Appearing in the third row of seven cards, these might tell you that more prosperous days are ahead after a difficult time (5 of Pentacles R) as you embark on a new job or career (the Fool). But pay attention (Knight of Swords)—this opportunity will come fast!

Your Mission Spread: The Future

This is the third and final row of cards that you lay down for your Mission Spread. It tells the story of the future and of what can happen as a result of the decisions and choices you make. If you've taken a detour from your path of purpose, these cards can point the way back.

Card 15: _____

Response: _____

Card 16: _____

Response: _____

Card 17: _____

Response: _____

Card 18: _____

Response: _____

Card 19: _____

Response: _____

Card 20: _____

Response: _____

Card 21: _____

Response: _____

Overall perspective and comments:

_____

_____

chapter 9

Create Your Success Resumé

Tarot's genie
Will you get your wish?
A little solar power to light up your houses
The face of your career of bliss
Influences of the outer planets
The Fool embarks on a journey of lifework

As one journey ends, another begins. You've traveled the pages of this book, using the Intuitive Arts to explore your career potential. You've used Astrology, Psychic Intuition, and Tarot to gain insights and understanding about the support the universe provides for your talents and abilities—and the challenges you might encounter along your path to career bliss. You've investigated your relationships with co-workers and your job or company, and likely have a good idea whether you can reshape your current job to align with what you've learned about your interests and your needs, or if it's time to move on to other opportunities. Your next journey—the quest to find and follow your lifework—is about to begin. You're ready to prepare your resumé and launch your success!

Make a Wish

Wouldn't it be great to rub the cover of this book and have a genie appear to grant you one career wish? We wish we could make that happen! Although the 9 of Cups card isn't exactly a genie, it is the Tarot's Wish Card. When the 9 of Cups appears in any Tarot reading, rejoice! This card represents the culmination of your desires and achievements. Of course, we and you know that reaching such a pinnacle is the result of focus and effort—although a gentle push from Jupiter ♃, the planet of good fortune, doesn't hurt.

The 9 of Cups is the Tarot's Wish Card. Whenever it shows up in a Tarot reading, your desires are within reach!

The Tarot's Wish Spread lets you ask if your wish will come true. The more specific your question, the more reliable the information that comes to you in response. You might ask:

- ☯ *"I wish I would get the job in accounting. Will I?"*
- ☯ *"I wish I could start my own business. Is that in my future?"*
- ☯ *"I wish I could find a part-time job so I could go back to school. Will that happen?"*

You have a lot of wishes about your job and career; the Wish Spread draws 15 cards to give you insights into the conditions and circumstances surrounding your desires. Some factors are beyond your ability to influence or control, and the Wish Spread can help you identify what they are so you can figure out what to do to make the most of them. Many other factors are matters of timing—being in the right place and the right time, knowing who to approach and who supports you, opening doors of opportunity.

To do a Wish Spread, first let your Psychic Intuition choose a card, any card, to represent you. This card goes face up in the center of the spread. After you've picked your card, shuffle the rest of the cards while focusing on your wish. When you're ready, put the deck of cards down on the table and fan them out. Randomly select 15 cards—don't look at them! Keep them face down.

When you've picked your 15 cards, set aside the rest of the deck. Shuffle these 15 cards until you're ready to lay them out. Then place them, face up, in the order the illustration shows.

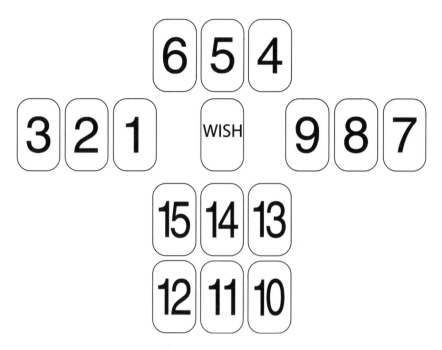

For the Tarot Wish Spread, lay out your cards in this order. The "W" is the card you selected to represent yourself.

Like most Tarot spreads, the Wish Spread tells a story about your question and it's up to you to interpret the meaning in the context of your circumstances and situation. Look at the cards in their groups of three. Consider each card individually, as well as in relationship to the other cards in the group. Then look at the overall story of the reading. Make sure to note whether a card appears reversed; a reversed card often suggests delays, reconsiderations, or, of course, reversals of the card's upright meanings.

Let your Psychic Intuition guide your perceptions and interpretations. Take your time; this is a complex reading and there often are many subtleties and nuances to the relationships among the cards. Remember, cards can represent people, situations, events, places, circumstances—and they can be literal or symbolic.

Write the cards of your Wish Spread, and your perceptions about the story they tell, here.

Card you chose to represent you: _____

Why:

_____

Cards 1, 2, and 3. These cards tell why you're making this wish.

Card 1: _____   Card 2: _____   Card 3: _____

Perceptions: _____

Cards 4, 5, and 6. These cards tell what your wish is, or what you hope to accomplish through your wish.

Card 4: _____   Card 5: _____   Card 6: _____

Perceptions: _____

Cards 7, 8, and 9. These cards show what might be standing in the way of your wish coming true, or what obstacles or challenges you must first confront.

Card 7: _____   Card 8: _____   Card 9: _____

Perceptions: _____

Cards 10, 11, and 12. These cards tell you whether your wish will come true.

Card 10: _____   Card 11: _____   Card 12: _____

Perceptions: _____

Cards 13, 14, and 15. These cards show what will come into your life or what changes are in store for you.

Card 13: _____   Card 14: _____   Card 15: _____

Perceptions: _____

Overall perceptions and comments:

_____

_____

Is there a particular card that confuses you, or seems out of place with the rest of the cards? Hold that card in your hands and reflect on it. Let your Psychic Intuition explore the card's range of meaning and symbolism without interference from your thinking brain. Does the reading suggest your wish will come true? What actions do you need to take to help it along? An abundance of Major Arcana cards suggests that the course is set through factors beyond your influence. When you draw mostly Minor Arcana cards, your wish depends on what you do.

Baby, Won't You Light My Fire: Sun ☉ Transits

When you were a kid, did you ever start a newspaper or pile of leaves on fire with a magnifying glass? A Sun ☉ transit is just like that, sharply focusing a sign's energy to create "combustion" in the sign's area of influence. The Sun is bright, hot, invigorating—and that's its effect when it visits a sign. The Sun stimulates and intensifies a sign's energy and influence.

As the Sun ☉ travels through your chart, it stays in each sign and its house of influence for a month. The most potent effect is when its visit conjuncts your natal Sun ☉ ♂ ☉. This is your solar return, a celestial "Happy Birthday!"

THE SUN .

Sun ☉ transits light up the full energy of an astrological sign and its house. Like the happy child basking in the warmth of the Sun's rays on the Tarot's Major Arcana card the Sun, open yourself to the potential!

When the Sun ☉ enters its native sign of Leo ♌, hang on! This alignment is like a solar flare, sending a burst of energy that can be overpowering and disruptive if you're not ready for it. And if Leo ♌ is your natal Sun ☉, you can be unstoppable when your ruling planet stops by for a cosmic visit. This puts a lot of fire in your hands ... use it wisely, or it'll burn you!

Sun ☉ In	Element	Supportive Energy	Good Time To
Aries ♈ *Emperor*	Fire	Confidence, invincibility, passion, exuberance	Compete for a plum assignment, promotion, or new job
Taurus ♉ *Hierophant*	Earth	Persistence, commitment, tenacity, determination	Complete projects, establish productive routines, put plans and ideas into action
Gemini ♊ *Lovers*	Air	Articulation, wit, humor, sharing, flexibility	Make presentations, speak in public, present ideas and plans to higher-ups
Cancer ♋ *Temperance*	Water	Sensitivity, emotion, compassion, nurturing	Form work partnerships, engage in team-building activities, bolster relationships with coworkers
Leo ♌ *Strength*	Fire	Strength, vigor, self-confidence, boldness	Host an open house, seminar, or other event that showcases individual or company capabilities
Virgo ♍ *Hermit*	Earth	Focus, concentration, logic, planning	Establish priorities and goals, put structures in place to support them
Libra ♎ *Justice*	Air	Deliberation, assessment, diplomacy, caution	Collect and evaluate opinions, information, and data
Scorpio ♏ *Judgement*	Water	Clarity, investigation, intensity, truth	Frank assessment that cuts to the essence of the situation, uncovering hidden agendas
Sagittarius ♐ *Chariot*	Fire	Innovation, adventure, risk, optimism	Develop new methods and routines, implement improvements
Capricorn ♑ *World*	Earth	Efficiency, concentration, patience, self-control	Do things right rather than just getting them done

Sun ☉ In	Element	Supportive Energy	Good Time To
Aquarius ♒ *Star*	Air	Originality, imagination, vision, intellect	Synchronize personal, work, group, and company goals
Pisces ♓ *High Priestess*	Water	Introspection, reflection, intuition, open-mindedness	Evaluate progress and direction

You can use an astrological calendar to determine the current Sun ☉ transit. Or you can make an educated guess just by looking at a regular calendar and a list of the dates of the Zodiac signs. Whatever is the sign of the current date, that's the sign of the Sun's transit. For example, if today is December 12, the Sun is transiting Sagittarius ♐. If it's May 6, the Sun is in Taurus ♉.

The Sun ☉ energizes the planets and their houses that are in the sign of its transit. If you have Mercury ☿ in Sagittarius ♐ in your 5th house of creativity and the Sun is in Sagittarius, it's a great time to create a really knock-out resumé! Where is the Sun ☉ right now, and how is it influencing your birth chart?

Create a "Career of Bliss" Collage

For this Psychic Intuition exercise, you need a half-dozen or so magazines and newspapers that you can cut up, scissors, glue, a marker or crayon, a piece of posterboard, a flashlight, and two helpers. (Kids are great for this.) If you don't have posterboard, lay out six sheets of printer or copier paper, three across and two down (portrait orientation), and tape them together to create a paper the size of posterboard. Tape the full length of each seam so there are no gaps.

Tape the posterboard onto a wall at a height so that when you stand in front of it, your head fits within the borders of the paper. Got those helpers? Give one of them a flashlight and the other the marker or crayon. Turn down the lights in the room. Step in front of the posterboard and turn sideways.

Have your helper shine the flashlight so it casts your shadow, in profile, onto the posterboard—standing far enough from you so the circle of light from the flashlight creates a complete shadow of your profile. Move closer or farther so your profile fills the paper. (One of your helpers can guide you.)

Have your other helper trace the outline of your profile. If you're using posterboard, do the tracing with a marker. If you're using paper taped into the size of posterboard, do the tracing with a crayon as the marker could bleed through the paper onto the wall. (Not good!)

When your profile is complete, take the posterboard down and thank your helpers. They might be curious about what you're doing and want to hang around, but tell them you need to be alone for this next part. Take your profile, scissors, glue, and magazines and newspapers to someplace you can sit in quiet and without interruptions.

On journeys of Psychic Intuition, the Tarot's the Fool finds guidance through the High Priestess, leading to the insights that put the World's opportunities within reach.

The only rule for this next step is that you can't think. Put your Psychic Intuition in full control. Take three deep, cleansing breaths and ask your inner eye, your psychic Third Eye, to envision your career of bliss. From the magazines and newspapers, clip words, pictures, want ads—images that catch your inner eye's attention. Don't think about the images, just cut out those that appeal to you.

When you have no more magazines and newspapers to cut up, look at the items you clipped. Choose one that best represents your dream job or your career of bliss. Glue it onto the posterboard at your eyes. Metaphorically, it is now the "lens" through which your collage "sees." Pick up one item at a time from those that you cut out and, letting your Psychic Intuition guide you, glue it into place on the paper. Continue until everything you clipped is glued somewhere.

When your collage is complete, tape it onto the wall at eye level. First, step far enough back from it that all of the pieces blur together and all you see is the overall image. What does it look like to you? Are there patterns to the colors or types of images? What's the first thing that comes to your mind? Write a few comments here:

_____

_____

Now step closer. How does your perception of the overall image change? What is the first piece of the collage that draws your eye to it? Why? Does your collage make you think of your dream job or career? When you look at the elements of your collage, do you see them as the separate pieces you glued together or do they form a collective impression? Write a few comments here:

_____

_____

Hang your collage someplace where you see it every day—in your workspace or office, if that's practical. Or on the door of the fridge, next to the mirror or on the back of the door in the bathroom, on the wall behind your home computer. Then, every day you can see the "face" of your future.

Influences from Afar

Orbiting through the Zodiac at such distance from our home planet Earth that their transits influence entire generations are the three outer planets: Uranus ♅, Neptune ♆, and Pluto ♇. Their astrological energies are both intense and prolonged. Uranus, the planet of originality and unexpected change, stays in each sign and house for 7 years. Neptune, the planet of imagination and dreams, stays for 14 years. And the irregular orbit of Pluto causes this planet of inner growth to settle into a sign and house for as short as 12 years to as long as 31 years.

Your personal growth under the influence of these planetary energies takes place through your relationships with larger structures—your company, your community, society at large. Each planet's house placement shapes how you will use the planet's energy.

Uranus ♅ is the planet of innovation. It manifests as a desire, often intense, to break free from convention and tradition. Natal Uranus in your 6th house of work often supports nontraditional employment structures and jobs, particularly those that are autonomous. Uranus resists authority or organization. You learn through Uranus's energy to develop your unconventional ways.

Neptune ♆ is the planet of ideals. It manifests as the drive to satisfy your spiritual and intuitive needs. Natal Neptune in your 10th house of career draws you to explore the mysteries of the intangible. Often, people in careers such as acting, theater, music, and other arts have natal Neptune in the 10th house—like actor Matt Damon (whose birth chart is in Chapter 7) and musician Yo-Yo Ma (whose birth chart is in Chapter 4). Neptune can allow secrets and hidden agendas to flourish. You learn through Neptune's energy to develop your idealism.

Pluto ♀ is the planet of transformation. It manifests as intense pressure to follow the soul's journey. Natal Pluto in your 6th house of work can direct tremendous energy toward work efforts. Pluto renews and regenerates, although the process of out-with-the-old is often painful and difficult. You learn through Pluto's energy your ability to transcend societal traditions.

Do you have any of these three power planets in your 6th house or 10th house? If not, do any of these planets—Uranus ♅, Neptune ♆, Pluto ♀—form aspects with planets in your houses of work and career? They can have far-reaching influences, both supportive and challenging.

The birth charts of these talented actors Ben Affleck and Matt Damon show strong support from Neptune ♆, the planet of imagination, which resides in Ben Affleck's 5th house of creativity and Matt Damon's 10th house of career.

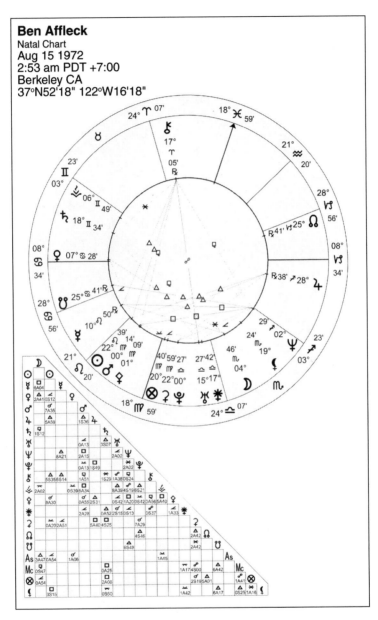

Ben Affleck
Natal Chart
Aug 15 1972
2:53 am PDT +7:00
Berkeley CA
37°N52'18" 122°W16'18"

Ben Affleck's birth chart.

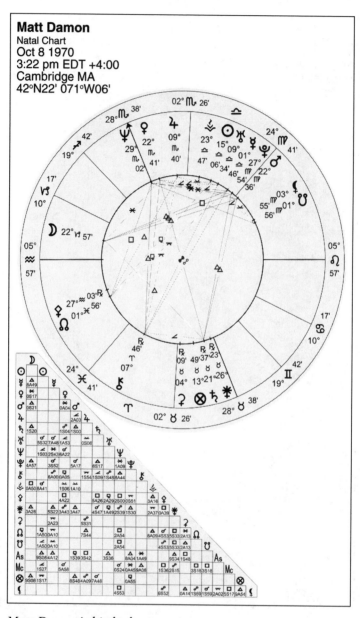

Matt Damon's birth chart.

Up Close and Personal

We've given you lots of suggestions for assessing your working relationships—with other people as well as with your job or your company. So we thought we'd try some of them out ourselves, and share our findings with you. As your co-authors, we—Arlene and Debbie— knew each other but hadn't worked together before collaborating to write this book.

We chose exercises that you, too, could do with your co-workers, business partners, or even your boss, with just some basic information about the other person. Now, because we share a common interest in understanding each other and our working relationship through the lens of the Intuitive Arts, we did exchange complete birth data—date, time, location—to provide the most accurate information.

But even when you don't have complete birth data, you can still get a pretty good idea of the compatibilities and challenges of your working relationships from using the information you can glean through casual conversation—generally birth date and birth location. Many workplaces celebrate or recognize birthdays, and most people enjoy talking about where they've lived ... an indirect route to asking the question, "So, where were you born?"

Reading the Signs

First, as we did with Bill Gates and Paul Allen in Chapter 3, we looked at our personal astrological signs—Sun ☉, Moon ☽, and ascendant— and added the descendant and midheaven to form a more complete picture. Here's what we found.

Arlene's Personal Astrological Signs

Planet or Point	Astro Sign	Element	Quality	Tarot Card
Sun ☉	Aquarius ♒	Air	Fixed	The Star
Moon ☽	Gemini ♊	Air	Mutable	The Lovers
Ascendant	Pisces ♓	Water	Mutable	High Priestess
Descendant	Virgo ♍	Earth	Mutable	The Hermit
Midheaven	Sagittarius ♐	Fire	Mutable	The Chariot

Debbie's Personal Astrological Signs

Planet or Point	Astro Sign	Element	Quality	Tarot Card
Sun ☉	Aries ♈	Fire	Cardinal	The Magician
Moon ☽	Leo ♌	Fire	Fixed	Strength
Ascendant	Scorpio ♏	Water	Fixed	Judgement
Descendant	Taurus ♉	Earth	Fixed	The Empress
Midheaven	Virgo ♍	Earth	Mutable	The Hermit

Look at all that "go-with-the-flow" Mutable energy in Arlene's signs to accommodate the Cardinal and Fixed energies in Debbie's signs! Arlene's versatile Gemini ♊ Moon ☽ is able to quickly and comfortably adapt to the push of Debbie's driving Cardinal Sun ☉ in Aries ♈.

The Tarot cards that correspond to the Sun ☉ and Moon ☽ signs of Arlene and Debbie.

In Chapter 5, we explored the compatibility between Bill Gates and Microsoft through the context of the Elements. Seeing immediately those interesting Air and Fire combinations in our Suns and Moons, we decided to create our Elemental formulas. To do this, we referred back to the table of Elemental combinations and their key traits in Chapter 5.

Planet	Elemental Combination	Elemental Key Traits	Elemental Nature
Sun ☉ *Identity*	Air + Fire	Thinks + acts	Supportive
Moon ☽ *Passion*	Air + Fire	Envisions + initiates	Supportive
Ascendant *Persona*	Water + Water	Intuits + creates	Conditional/ compatible

Planet	Elemental Combination	Elemental Key Traits	Elemental Nature
Descendant *Partnership*	Earth + Earth	Stabilizes + focuses	Conditional/ compatible
Midheaven *Career*	Fire + Earth	Leads + grounds	Challenging

To make a determination about the conditional nature of our ascendants, we looked at some of the other planetary placements in our respective birth charts. We also took advantage of Arlene's expertise and created a synastry grid to explore the aspects between our charts, just as we did for the far more famous writing team of Ben Affleck and Matt Damon in Chapter 7. If you don't know enough of the other person's information to do this in your comparisons, you can look at your own planetary placements in your birth chart for insights about your approaches, and put your Psychic Intuition to work to sense the approaches of your co-worker or business partner.

Arlene identified a trine △ aspecting our ascendants—a smooth, effortless flow of supportive energy. Arlene's ascendant conjuncts ☌ Debbie's Mercury ☿, the planet of communication. But Debbie's Mercury is in the sign of Pisces ♓—the same sign as Arlene's ascendant. So this is a favorable conjunction.

The challenging Elemental nature of our midheavens gave us pause, but only briefly. Although we have Fire and Earth, each is in a Mutable sign. There are no aspects between our midheavens, and mostly favorable aspects between our midheavens and planetary placements. Arlene's midheaven squares □ Debbie's Mercury ☿, suggesting that Debbie's communication style might not jibe with Arlene's approach to public recognition for her career goals. And Debbie's Virgo ♍ midheaven squares Arlene's Gemini ♊ Moon ☽—the need for organization confronts comfort with ambiguity.

This played itself out through occasional grappling to find middle ground in how we presented certain concepts in this book. Again, the Pisces ♓ influence on Debbie's Mercury ☿ and the Mutable energies of Arlene's ascendant and Moon ☽ helped to smooth the flow. What could have been some serious struggling instead worked out as collaborative effort. Remember, inside the challenge of a square □ is an opportunity! When you can identify and work through the challenge, the aspect becomes supportive.

A match made in the heavens? On an Elemental level, it appears so!

Reading the Cards

Next, we selected Tarot cards to represent ourselves and each other. Arlene chose the Magician and the 3 of Wands to represent Debbie and the Hermit and the 2 of Wands to represent herself. Debbie chose the Star and the Queen of Wands to represent Arlene, and the Wheel of Fortune and the Knight of Wands to represent herself. Interestingly, we picked the Major Arcana cards that correlate to our respective Sun ☉ signs to represent each other—the Magician is the card of Aries ♈, and the Star is the card of Aquarius ♒.

Arlene chose the Magician and the 3 of Wands to represent Debbie, and the Hermit and the 2 of Wands to represent herself.

Arlene's comments: "I feel the Magician represents Debbie's talents to reveal the technical skill of writing and humor she adds to the work. All of Debbie's tools are on her table of expertise, and like magic, the sentences flow. The 3 of Wands represents our working relationship because of her ability to produce under stress and evaluate the next step even when we get stuck on a concept or a phrase. She produces with enthusiasm that will greatly connect to the public. I appreciate the speed and technical knowledge of which she relates a serious subject matter and that sense of devotion to our process.

"I chose the Hermit to represent myself, because this writing we've done has made me dig deep into my own past knowledge of all the metaphysical tools. I wrote at night, when the air was quiet and only the cat walked across my keyboard! The 2 of Wands was certainly me, watching and waiting for the results of my knowledge being put to paper. I have an introspective side that tried to 'feel' and 'get energized' by how the public would read our work. Our partnership pulled to-gether the two of our energies to create the magic of writing and the spirit of service to others."

Debbie chose the Star and the Queen of Wands to represent Arlene, and the Wheel of Fortune and the Knight of Wands to represent herself.

Debbie's comments: "I feel the Star represents Arlene because, like the woman on the card, she draws from an endless source to offer the insights that give people hope and inspiration. Without glossing over challenges and difficulties, Arlene can find and pull out the positive. I chose the Queen of Wands to represent Arlene's approach to our working relationship because Arlene nurtures and gives guidance at the same time, encouraging others to grow in their own ways.

"I picked the Wheel of Fortune to represent myself in this partnership because it was a serendipitous cascade of events that made it possible for me to join Arlene in writing this book. And I chose the Knight of Wands to represent my approach to our working relationship because it's my nature to charge into adventures that take me into new territories—precisely is why I need and appreciate the kind and knowledgeable guidance of the Queen of Wands!"

If your co-worker or business partner is willing, you can do a similar exercise between the two of you. Each of you chooses a Major Arcana card to represent yourself and the other. Then select a Minor Arcana card to represent your respective approaches to the work you do together, again for yourself and for the other. Lay the cards out in various combinations. What impressions do you get? You can do this exercise by yourself, too, just by exploring the two sets of cards you choose to represent each of you.

Your Path to Bliss: Your Intuitive Arts Resumé

Now we're going to pick a Tarot card for you: the Fool, the first card of the Major Arcana. We choose the Fool because it represents the start of a grand and glorious journey for you, the quest to find and follow the path of your lifework, as you finish this book and apply what you've learned through the Intuitive Arts.

The Fool we talked about in Chapter 1 was uninformed and unaware—blissful, it appears, in the innocence of not knowing what challenges and even potential dangers lay ahead. That Fool is eager and carefree, setting off in search of opportunities. *What* opportunities, and *where* are they? The Fool of Chapter 1 doesn't know! That Fool knows only that opportunities are out there—they *have* to be.

The Fool of Chapter 9, having traveled the journey of this book and explored the Intuitive Arts, is informed and focused. This Fool strides forward with intent. Yes, there is a cliff, and yes, the next step is dangerously close to its edge. But so is opportunity, and this Fool knows just where to find it. Dangers the uninformed Fool of Chapter 1 might face don't apply to the Fool of Chapter 9—*this* Fool is ready to fly.

The World awaits the Fool!

And so, now, are you! Informed, aware, purposeful, you can harness the Fool's most beneficial energy on the journey of *your* lifework. You've used Astrology to learn the influences of the planets and signs. You've used Psychic Intuition to see past the clutter of your logical mind to the truth of your inner vision. And you've used Tarot to explore the stories of your work and life experiences in ways that shape and define them, revealing insights and understandings. You know where you want to go and how to get there, and you have a new set of tools to guide your way. Destination: the World!

appendix A

Success Stars

The wheel of the Zodiac
Planets in houses
Signs in houses
Planet personalities and rulers
House keywords
Sun sign and birth time
The signs of your ascendant, descendant, and midheaven
Letting your career path lead you to your bliss
Ordering birth charts and synastry grids online

*The energies of the astrological houses, signs, and planets influence
how you view and interact with the environment and people of your
personal world. How you use these energies determines how your life
unfolds. It is your destiny to succeed!*

The Wheel of the Zodiac

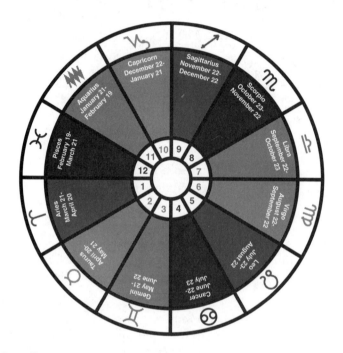

By the Signs

Here's a quick, handy reference to the astrological signs.

Aries, the Ram ♈	**March 21 to April 20**
Element	Fire
Quality	Cardinal
Energy	*Yang*
Rulers	Mars and Pluto
Anatomy	Brain, eyes, face
Keywords	Pioneering, initiating, beginnings

Taurus, the Bull ♉	**April 20 to May 21**
Element	Earth
Quality	Fixed
Energy	*Yin*
Ruler	Venus
Anatomy	Neck, throat, thyroid
Keywords	Ownership, dependability, sensuality

Gemini, the Twins ♊ May 21 to June 22

Element	Air
Quality	Mutable
Energy	*Yang*
Ruler	Mercury
Anatomy	Hands, arms, shoulders, lungs
Keywords	Mentality, communication, versatility

Cancer, the Crab ♋ June 22 to July 23

Element	Water
Quality	Cardinal
Energy	*Yin*
Ruler	Moon
Anatomy	Stomach, breasts
Keywords	Feeling, sensitivity, nurturing

Leo, the Lion ♌ July 23 to August 22

Element	Fire
Quality	Fixed
Energy	*Yang*
Ruler	Sun
Anatomy	Back, spine, heart
Keywords	Willpower, creativity, expressing the heart

Virgo, the Virgin ♍ August 22 to September 22

Element	Earth
Quality	Mutable
Energy	*Yin*
Ruler	Mercury
Anatomy	Intestines and colon
Keywords	Service, self-improvement, sacred patterns

Libra, the Scales ♎ September 22 to October 23

Element	Air
Quality	Cardinal
Energy	*Yang*
Ruler	Venus
Anatomy	Kidneys, lower back, adrenal glands
Keywords	Balance, harmony, justice

Scorpio, the Scorpion ♏

October 23 to November 22

Element	Water
Quality	Fixed
Energy	*Yin*
Rulers	Pluto and Mars
Anatomy	Genitals, urinary and reproductive systems
Keywords	Desire, transformation, power

Sagittarius, the Archer ♐

November 22 to December 22

Element	Fire
Quality	Mutable
Energy	*Yang*
Ruler	Jupiter
Anatomy	Liver, hips, thighs
Keywords	Understanding, enthusiasm, exploration

Capricorn, the Goat ♑

December 22 to January 21

Element	Earth
Quality	Cardinal
Energy	*Yin*
Ruler	Saturn
Anatomy	Bones, joints, knees, teeth
Keywords	Achievement, structure, organization

Aquarius, the Water Bearer ♒

January 21 to February 19

Element	Air
Quality	Fixed
Energy	*Yang*
Rulers	Uranus and Saturn
Anatomy	Ankles, circulation
Keywords	Humanitarian, unique, innovative

Pisces, the Fishes ♓

February 19 to March 21

Element	Water
Quality	Mutable
Energy	*Yin*

Pisces, the Fishes ♓	February 19 to March 21
Rulers	Neptune and Jupiter
Anatomy	Feet, immune system, hormonal system
Keywords	Compassion, universality, inclusiveness

By the Planets

Here's a quick, handy reference to the energy of each planet.

Planet	Symbol	Energies	Action Keyword
Sun	☉	Self, essence, life spirit, creativity, willpower	Explores
Moon	☽	Emotions, instincts, unconscious, past memories	Senses
Mercury	☿	Mental activities, communication, intelligence	Communicates
Venus	♀	Love, art, beauty, social graces, harmony, money, resources, possessions	Enjoys
Mars	♂	Physical energy, boldness, warrior ways, action, desires anger, courage, ego	Acts
Jupiter	♃	Luck, abundance, wisdom, higher education, philosophy or beliefs, exploration, growth	Benefits
Saturn	♄	Responsibilities, self-discipline, perseverance, limitations, structures	Works
Uranus	♅	Sudden or unexpected change, originality, liberation, radical thinking, authenticity	Innovates
Neptune	♆	Idealism, subconscious, spirituality, intuition, clairvoyance	Dreams
Pluto	♇	Power, regeneration, destruction, rebirth, transformation	Transforms

Signs in Houses

House	Astro Sign
1st	Aries ♈
2nd	Taurus ♉
3rd	Gemini ♊
4th	Cancer ♋
5th	Leo ♌
6th	Virgo ♍
7th	Libra ♎
8th	Scorpio ♏
9th	Sagittarius ♐
10th	Capricorn ♑
11th	Aquarius ♒
12th	Pisces ♓

Planetary Rulers

Planet	Signs Ruled
Sun ☉	Leo ♌
Moon ☽	Cancer ♋
Mercury ☿	Gemini ♊, Virgo ♍
Venus ♀	Taurus ♉, Libra ♎
Mars ♂	Aries ♈, co-ruler of Scorpio ♏
Jupiter ♃	Sagittarius ♐, co-ruler of Pisces ♓
Saturn ♄	Capricorn ♑, co-ruler of Aquarius ♒
Uranus ♅	Aquarius ♒
Neptune ♆	Pisces ♓
Pluto ♇	Scorpio ♏, co-ruler of Aries ♈

House Keywords

House	Keyword(s)
1st	Identity and self
2nd	Self-worth and values
3rd	Knowledge and communication
4th	Home and family
5th	Creativity
6th	Work and service

House	Keyword(s)
7th	Relationships and partnerships
8th	Transformation
9th	Beliefs and philosophy
10th	Ethics and career
11th	Community, humanitarianism
12th	Spirituality, secrets

Your Ascendant, Descendant, and Midheaven

Certain points on your birth chart have special influence when it comes to matters of work and career.

- **Ascendant.** Located on the cusp of your 1st house of self, your ascendant reflects the "outward" you. It is the sign that was rising on the eastern horizon at the moment of your birth. This is the part of you that people see when they first meet you, the part of yourself you present to the public. Your ascendant influences your personality and your physical appearance.
- **Descendant.** Your descendant marks the cusp of your 7th house of partnerships, directly across the horizon of your birth chart from your ascendant. It is the sign that was setting on the western horizon at the moment of your birth, and reflects what you perceive as lacking in yourself. Your descendant influences the way you partner with others to accommodate these needs.
- **Midheaven.** Your midheaven is the sign on the cusp of your 10th house of career. It influences and reflects how you approach your career. It also represents your public reputation, showing how well you connect the tasks of your job (your 6th house) with the path of your career (your 10th house). The stronger this connection, the closer the perceptions of others to your perception of yourself.

Asteroids and Planetoids

More than just the planets move through your birth chart! Here are the asteroids, the planetoid Chiron, and their areas of influence.

Asteroid	Realm	Areas of Influence
Ceres ⚳	Motherhood	Natural cycles, fertility, crops, relationships between parents and children
Juno ⚵	Marriage	Partnerships, contracts and agreements, social obligations
Pallas Athene ⚴	Wisdom	Intelligence, knowledge, understanding, equality
Vesta ⚶	Power	Sexuality, devotion, health, service to others
Planetoid		
Chiron ⚷	Healing	Transformation, personal growth

Aspects

Aspects are the geometric relationships between any two planets in your own chart, as well as in relation to another chart, whether for another person, a moment in time, or your own progressed chart. The main aspects to consider are:

- ☽ **Conjunction** ☌   The strongest aspects. In a conjunction, the planets are placed at the same point in a chart or charts. Conjunctions are considered a focal point, with the interaction of the two planets emphasized.
- ☽ **Sextile** ✶   In a sextile, the planets are 60° apart. The signs in a sextile share the same energy (*yin* or *yang*), so this is considered to be a favorable aspect.
- ☽ **Square** □   In a square, the planets are 90° apart. Although squares are considered to be chart challenges, they often provide the impetus for change and improvement.
- ☽ **Trine** △   In a trine, the planets are 120° apart. This most favorable of the aspects means the planets share both element and energy. Trines indicate positive connections, often made so easily you may not even notice.
- ☽ **Opposition** ☍   In an opposition, the planets are 180° apart. There's little in common with an opposition, but, like squares, their difficult energy can spur us on to meet challenges.
- ☽ **Quincunx** ⚻   In a quincunx, the planets are 150° apart. Quincunxes are interesting—nothing is shared between the two signs, so some adjustment is usually required in order for them to interact.

Astrological Extras

The astrological charts and grids you see as examples throughout this book contain two symbols we don't include in our discussions but that might interest you in your further explorations of Astrology. These are the Part of Fortune ⊗ and the minor asteroid Lilith ⚸. The Part of Fortune, sometimes called the Lot of Fortune, derives from ancient Astrology and represents the intersection in the Zodiac where your Sun ☉, Moon ☽, and ascendant converge. The Part of Fortune in its basic symbolism is a "point of karmic reward" in your birth chart. The ancients believed the Part of Fortune is what you would receive as a cosmic gift as you grew in this lifetime. Lilith, also called the Dark Moon, represents primal and emotional connections to your shadow side, and "liberation from conformity" in present-day interpretations.

Finding Your Career Path and Your Bliss

Work is everywhere on your birth chart, but there are a few special places that will give you a quick assessment of where you are on your career path. We've used Bruce Springsteen's birth chart and numbered the areas to pay special attention to when you're looking for success. We've also cross-referenced the chapter that covers this area in detail.

1. In Chapter 1, we showed you where to look for your Sun ☉, your expression of potential, and your Moon ☽, your expression of inner emotions. We also peeked into your 2nd house of values to take a look at the talents and resources you bring to your work, and how you'll use them to earn income throughout your career.

2. Also in Chapter 1, we introduced you to Mercury ☿, your way of communicating; Venus ♀, how you approach values and resources; Mars ♂, how you engage; and your ascendant, the mask you wear for the world.

3. In Chapter 2, you learned about the balance of *yin* and *yang* in your work and in your life. We explored the connections between your 4th house of home, 6th house of work, and 10th house of career to help you look at your balance between work and life. We also introduced you to aspects.

4. In Chapter 3, we introduced you to the Elements (Fire, Earth, Air, and Water) and Qualities (Cardinal, Fixed, Mutable). You identified how many personal signs you have with these attributes.

5. In Chapter 4, you learned how to look at your personal signs and planets and their houses to determine your approach to work.

6. In Chapter 5, we introduced you to synastry, the Astrology of relationships, and showed you how to use a synastry grid to assess your compatibility with your job or company.

7. Also in Chapter 5, we explained more about how your Elemental nature and the Qualities of your energies can help you determine whether you and your job or company are a good match.

8. In Chapter 6, we walked the Moon ☽ through the signs. We also looked at lunar cycles, Saturn ♄ returns, and planetary transits, so that you could find times when your birth chart might be generating job change and career development.

9. In Chapter 7, we introduced you to the asteroids, Ceres ⚳, Juno ⚵, Pallas Athene ⚴, and Vesta ⚶. We also introduced you to Chiron ⚷, the wounded healer, whose sign in your birth chart shows your own particular psychic wounds—your fears and worries—and your potential for healing.

10. Also in Chapter 7, we showed you how to use synastry to explore aspects in more depth, including the conjunction ☌, sextile ✶, square □, trine △, opposition ☍, and quincunx ⚻. We also revealed how certain more difficult aspects can challenge work partnerships involving other people or companies.

11. In Chapter 8, we explored Saturn ♄, the Nodes ☋ ☊, and the 11th house in more detail to help you synchronize your career path with the path of your life goals and ideals.

12. Finally, in Chapter 9, we showed you how to enlist the energies of solar transits, the outer planets, and your Psychic Intuition to start a new job, transition to a new career, or launch a new business or venture.

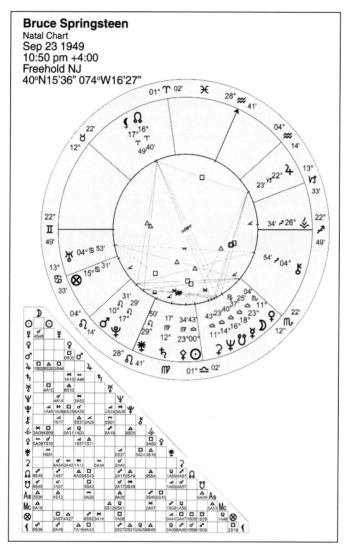

Bruce Springsteen
Natal Chart
Sep 23 1949
10:50 pm +4:00
Freehold NJ
40°N15'36" 074°W16'27"

Bruce Springsteen's birth chart and aspect grid.

Ordering Birth Charts and Synastry Grids Online

Several websites will do birth charts for you. To get a birth chart that you can use with this book, be sure to specify that you want Geocentric, Tropical Zodiac, Placidus house system, and True Node. Check out Arlene's site at www.mellinetti.com. Also check out Astrolabe, Inc., at www.alabe.com—this is the company that publishes Solar Fire, the computer software program Arlene used to generate the birth charts we used as examples throughout this book. A few other good astrology websites include www.astro.com, www.astrodatabank.com, and www. stariq.com. But there are many astrological sites on the Internet; explore and choose the site that resonates to you and your investigation of Astrology, the heavens, and your *working* place in the universe.

Birth Time and Your Birth Chart

The position of the Sun ☉ in the heavens at the time of your birth determines the placement of the planets and signs in the houses of your astrological birth chart. To know the precise position of the Sun, you need to know the location, date, and time of your birth. Many people don't know their birth times. There are various methods astrologers can use to cast birth charts when this is the case.

For the birth charts with unknown birth times that we used in this book, Arlene used the method called "noon chart." A noon chart uses noon as your time of birth, placing your Sun ☉ at the apex of the horoscope wheel—on your midheaven. Symbolically, this puts your soul at its highest potential in this lifetime, looking down with an eagle's-eye view, so to speak, on the planets and how they "fall" into place in the astrological houses to represent your life. Although there are some imprecisions with this or any method of casting a birth chart without a precise time of birth (for example, the ascendant sign changes every two hours), Arlene finds the noon chart allows the most accurate interpretations for the broadest range of people.

appendix B

Success Cards

No Tarot card's meaning is absolute, and for that reason, we encourage you to make personal interpretations of the cards, both by studying their individual images, and examining the stories told by the cards' interrelationships. The images you see here are from the Universal Waite Tarot Deck published by U.S. Game Systems, Inc.

At the same time, knowing the traditional meanings of the cards can often give you an additional spin you might not have considered in your initial interpretation. That's why we've taken a fresh look at the cards' meanings as they apply specifically to work and career.

Tarot's Major Arcana

The Fool
New opportunities
Endless possibilities
Fresh approaches

The Fool R
Uncertainty
A wrong direction
Look before you leap!

*The Magician
The power to
manifest desire
Ask and ye shall
receive
A creative or
inventive person*

*The Magician R
Possibility of
manipulation
Lack of follow-
through
A user or abuser*

*The High
Priestess
Intuition and
inner knowing
Yin and yang—
emotions + logic
Mentor*

*The High
Priestess R
Dream or illusion
A hidden agenda
Lack of insight*

*The Empress
Abundance and
potential
Harmony in rela-
tionships
An environment
for growth and
prosperity*

*The Empress R
Disagreements
and contention
Emphasis on
appearances
Facade rather
than structure*

The Emperor
Paternal author-
ity figure
Past experience
can guide the
present
Self-discipline

The Emperor R
Insecurity
Stubbornness
Self-centeredness

The Hierophant
A traditional job
or career
Staying between
the lines
A solid spiritual
foundation

The Hierophant R
An unconventional
approach to work
A risk-taker
A relationship with
freedom

The Lovers
A new partner-
ship or job
Good start for a
relationship
Peaceful coexis-
tence

The Lovers R
Separation or
division
Obstacles to
desires
A need for better
communication

The Chariot
Ability to meet
challenges
Focus and deter-
mination to
achieve goal
Positive outcome
after difficult
time

The Chariot R
Confusion
Someone else in
control
A battle not
worth fighting

Strength
Inner strength
and courage
Love without fear
The power of
gentle persuasion

Strength R
A power struggle
Intense emotions
that can lead to
upset
Uncontrolled
ambitions

The Hermit
Introspection and
solitude
A desire for truth
Trust own inner
voice for guid-
ance

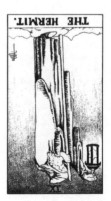

The Hermit R
Inability to see
clearly
Wishing instead
of acting
A reminder to
pay attention to
past lessons

The Wheel of
Fortune
Destiny comes
calling!
Serendipitous
circumstances
A golden oppor-
tunity comes
around

The Wheel of
Fortune R
What goes up
must come down
Events beyond
control
A grinding halt

Justice
Fairness and a
desire for balance
A legal agreement
or contract
Universal laws
will prevail

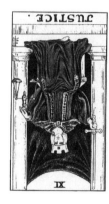

Justice R
Unwise counsel
Conditions that
are out of balance
Unable to see the
whole picture

The Hanged Man
Desire for a differ-
ent lifestyle
At a crossroads
A lack of motion—
feeling "stuck"

The Hanged Man R
Inability to give up
old lifestyle
Inability to make a
decision
Fear of change

*Death
The end of the
old makes way
for new
A catalyst for
change
A new dawn*

*Death R
Past blockages
impede progress
Stagnation and
stalemate
Arguments; too
tired to care*

*Temperance
Balance
Giving and taking
in equal measure
The importance
of moderation*

*Temperance R
Impatience
and pushiness
Inability to listen
to others
Being taken
advantage of*

*The Devil
Obsession or ad-
dictive behaviors
Materialistic
focus
Wrong applica-
tion of force,
aggression*

*The Devil R
Freedom from fear
Ability to unlock
own chains
A burden lifted*

*The Tower
Unexpected events
Collapse of a
faulty foundation
Don't depend too
much on systems
and devices*

*The Tower R
A surprising nuance
to a situation
Pay attention to
intuitive nudges
Renewed faith after
difficult life change*

*The Star
Optimism
and faith
What you need
is here
Successful per-
formance*

*The Star R
Insecurity
Lack of recognition
for achievements
A feeling of loss—
not always
warranted*

*The Moon
Emotions at
full force
Trust your psy-
chic intuition
Major changes
coming*

*The Moon R
Understanding
after initial
confusion
Focused innova-
tion and creativity
Truth emerges*

The Sun
Achieving goals
Prospects
and the future
look bright
Joy and satis-
faction

The Sun R
Partnership
problems
Lack of direction
Cloudy forecast

Judgement
A new under-
standing of past
lessons "I can see
clearly now!"
An awakening to
cosmic awareness

Judgement R
At a crossroads
Fears holding
you back
Frustrating delays

The World
Successful
culmination
Your new life-
style is ready!
Freedom to do
as you desire

The World R
A bit more work is
needed to achieve
goal
Life—and career—
is what you make it
You're almost
there!

Tarot's Minor Arcana

Ace of Wands
A fresh start or
new direction
The first step
toward creating
your passion
A new job or
promotion

Ace of Wands R
Overenthusiasm
gets in your way
Delays or
frustration
Pushiness or
aggression

2 of Wands
Waiting for
results
A good per-
spective
A positive
attitude

2 of Wands R
Lack of follow-
through
Delays because
of others
A hidden agenda

3 of Wands
Cooperation and
partnership
Good results
forthcoming
Plans set in
motion

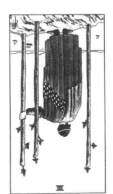

3 of Wands R
Wasted energy
Inadequate
resources
No one in
the lead

4 of Wands
A celebration
Happiness
and success
A dream come
true

4 of Wands R
Life's little joys
Harmonious
meeting or event
Enjoying small
successes

5 of Wands
Lack of
teamwork
Disagreement
and crossed
purposes
Aggression
and misplaced
energies

5 of Wands R
A win-win
situation
Compromise
and cooperation
Negotiation and
constructive talks

6 of Wands
Return after
success
All efforts come
together
Visitors arriving

6 of Wands R
Stressful
conditions
Need to ride
out the storm
Just not your day

7 of Wands
Anxiety
and worry
Uncertain or
unclear priorities
Limited or inade-
quate resources

7 of Wands R
The storm is
passing
A sense of
personal
empowerment
Difficulties are
over

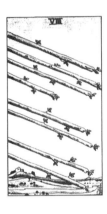

8 of Wands
The arrows of
opportunity are
arriving!
Shared passions
Common goals
and ideals

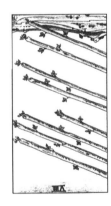

8 of Wands R
Disagreement
and discontent
Jealousy or envy
Work group
disputes

9 of Wands
Safeguarding
work and efforts
Forewarned is
forearmed
Well prepared to
handle crisis

9 of Wands R
Vulnerable
and tired
Desire to be
left alone
Anxiety and
poor health

Page of Wands
An exciting
message
An encouraging
companion
Good tidings
arrive

10 of Wands
Helping too many
others at once
Stressful work
conditions
Overwhelming
obligations

10 of Wands R
Shifting the burden
Learning to delegate
Taking the right
approach to
responsibility

Page of Wands
An exciting
message
An encouraging
companion
Good tidings
arrive

Page of Wands R
Disappointing news
Delay in receiving
expected information
A preoccupied young
person

Knight of Wands
Enthusiasm and
renewed energy
A new adventure
A co-worker you
can count on

Knight of Wands R
Postponed journey
Jealousy, arrogance,
or self-doubt
An unstable person

Queen of Wands
In command of
work resources
and systems
Someone who
encourages others'
self-sufficiency
Feminine ambition

Queen of Wands R
Discomfort in
the workplace
Possessive and
domineering
behavior
Confusion and
obstinacy

King of Wands
Someone willing
to lend a helping
hand
A good leader
in a crisis
A passionate
mentor

King of Wands R
Lack of confidence
Feeling grumpy
and detached
Pessimism or doubt

Ace of Pentacles
Beginning of pros-
perity and success
Confidence in
abilities
Happiness of solid
foundation

Ace of Pentacles R
Frustration
and delays
Need to hold tight
to what you have
Need to reassess
priorities

2 of Pentacles
Juggling multiple
interests and
responsibilities
Confidence
despite stress
Balance is essential

2 of Pentacles R
A hard time decid-
ing something
Need to simplify;
let something go
Need for caution

3 of Pentacles
A time to learn
new things
Approval for
work and talent
An award or
honor

3 of Pentacles R
The reality
doesn't look
like the plan
Lack of passion
Sloppy workman-
ship

4 of Pentacles
Holding tight to
what you have
Conservative
about money
Tight resources

4 of Pentacles R
Spending more
than you have
Use caution
when spending
Generosity;
overly generous

5 of Pentacles
A deep sense of
personal loss
Feelings of
separation
Limited work
opportunities

5 of Pentacles R
Renewed hope and
optimism after loss
Negative cycle ends
Can now reap what
was sown

6 of Pentacles
Extra help
is offered
Sharing with
others
Financial reward;
a new job

6 of Pentacles R
Be cautious of
what others offer
More giving
than taking
Bribery and
chicanery

7 of Pentacles
Self-confidence
Payment for
your skill
Financial inde-
pendence

7 of Pentacles R
Poor speculation
Problems with
land or real estate
A need for caution
when speculating

8 of Pentacles
Social approval
Development
of greater skill
Recognition for
job well done

8 of Pentacles R
Delayed production
Lack of balance
in personal life
Someone's burning
out

9 of Pentacles
Enjoying fruits
of labors
Self-sufficiency
and independence
Prosperity to
share

9 of Pentacles R
Financial insecurity
Shaken foundations
Uncertainty about
future

10 of Pentacles
Balance in life
Job security
A stable and
content future

10 of Pentacles R
Work group
discord
Assets and
resources at risk
Be cautious with
investments

Page of Pentacles
An eager learner
A message of
happiness
Good news—
good results

Page of Pentacles R
A selfish or demand-
ing child or person
Differing values
Prejudice or rebellion

Knight of Pentacles
Steady effort
pays off
Development of
prosperous future
Wise counsel and
good stewardship

Knight of Pentacles R
Discontent with
present work
Lack of guidance
and support
Trying to keep up
with the Joneses

Queen of Pentacles
A kind, gentle
person
Garden of success
Always something
in the works

Queen of Pentacles R
A needy or dependent
person
A lack of confidence
Losses in the home

King of Pentacles
A pragmatic leader
Assured prosperity
Someone who will
share the wealth

King of Pentacles R
Laziness or lack
of motivation
Ill equipped for
financial success
Disorganization,
discontent about
money

Ace of Swords
A new situation
A new way of
communicating
A sword can cut
two ways

Ace of Swords R
The need to be
cautious and vigilant
Beware of aggres-
sion or force
Listen before acting

2 of Swords
Disconnected
from emotions
Indecision or
stalemate
Need to concen-
trate and focus

2 of Swords R
Remember to con-
nect to intuition
Use caution to
maintain balance
Freedom to make
own decisions

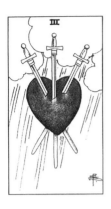

3 of Swords
Heartbreak and
sorrow
Pain and grief
Crisis and loss

3 of Swords R
Passing sadness
Dissatisfaction,
but all is not lost
A different result
than what was
expected

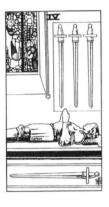

4 of Swords
R&R required!
Need for retreat
and meditation
Inner work being
done

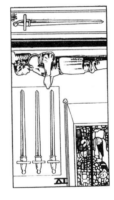

4 of Swords R
Ready for
renewed action
Ready to fight
for own rights
Opportunity to
change existing
condition

5 of Swords
Legal or contract
problems
Someone taking
unfair advantage
Loss, possible
slander

5 of Swords R
Feeling too
weak to fight
Discovering
deceit
The truth, how-
ever difficult,
will out

6 of Swords
Moving toward
calm and harmony
Unpleasant situa-
tion is resolving
Leaving regrets or
problems behind

6 of Swords R
Stuck in a diffi-
cult situation
Better to wait
and see
Learn to be
patient

7 of Swords
Someone's
being sneaky
A need for the
truth to come out
Contradictions
and duality

7 of Swords R
Wise counsel
will return
What was hidden
will be revealed
Freedom to
move on

8 of Swords
Bound by
own fears
Self-limiting
thoughts and
behaviors
Are you hurting
yourself the
most?

8 of Swords R
Letting go of fear
Facing one's
own restrictions
Ability to move
about freely once
more

9 of Swords
Difficult situations
Learning to deal
with loss and
regret
Emotional depres-
sion

9 of Swords R
The nightmare
is over
Negative energy
is dissipating now
The light at the
end of the tunnel

10 of Swords
End of a karmic
pattern
Leaving a
difficult job
Deep sense of
loss or separation

10 of Swords R
Releasing of a
karmic debt
Prepared to
move ahead
End of long,
stressful cycle

Page of Swords
Courage when
needed most
Using common-
sense approach
Pay attention to
details

Page of Swords R
Overly emotional
communication
Need to speak
mind
Importance of
truth

*Knight of Swords
Sudden change
of direction
Direct honesty—
sometimes
too direct
Full speed ahead!*

*Knight of Swords R
Out of control!
Arguments and dis-
ruptive behavior
Lack of emotional
insight*

*Queen of Swords
Ability to get to
heart of matter
Joy of debate
Honesty and
forthrightness*

*Queen of Swords R
Overly critical
person
Anxiety and mis-
communication
Judgmental or con-
tentious behavior*

*King of Swords
Logical analysis
Ability to probe
beneath surface
Rational counsel*

*King of Swords R
Preconceptions
without basis
Stubbornness and
unfair judgment
Selfishness or
aloofness*

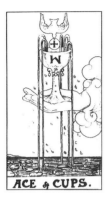

Ace of Cups
Opening yourself
to joy and
happiness
Start of a new
venture
Abundant
resources and
support

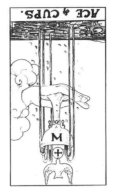

Ace of Cups R
Insecurity
Inability to con-
nect with others
Too much focus
on self

2 of Cups
Mutual under-
standing
Partnership or
joint venture
Developing
friendship

2 of Cups R
Need for
cooperation
Negative emotions
Jealousy or
possessiveness

3 of Cups
The honeymoon
phase
Happiness all
around
Cause for
celebration

3 of Cups R
Unhappiness
not being com-
municated
Pettiness,
overindulgence
Need to check
emotions

4 of Cups
The thrill is gone
Fantasy more
interesting
than reality
Nothing seems
right

4 of Cups R
Emotionally ready
to love again
Ready to recon-
nect with others
Ability to visual-
ize and create joy
in work

5 of Cups
Loss of job or
opportunity
Things not turn-
ing out as you
planned
Need to regroup
and refocus

5 of Cups R
Return of positive
energy and hope
Letting go of
negativity
Knowledge gained
through challenge

6 of Cups
Nostalgia for
the "good old
days"
A past oppor-
tunity returns
Sharing pros-
perity

6 of Cups R
Hurtful past
situation has
current echoes
Emotional need
to seek out past
Wishing for the
past instead of
the present

7 of Cups
Too many
choices!
Pay attention to
what's beneath
Indecisiveness

7 of Cups R
The fog has lifted
A plan has been
made
You finally took
action!

8 of Cups
Following the
call to a higher
mission
Leaving the
past behind
Seeking fulfill-
ment

8 of Cups R
New approaches
now possible
Time to follow
your bliss
Taking pleasure in
life's good things

9 of Cups
Happy days
are here!
Your wish will
come true
A new job or
career

9 of Cups R
Expecting
too much
Wishes postponed
A need to develop
patience

*10 of Cups
All that you've
worked for is
now yours
Beyond your
wildest dreams
Joy and happiness
in abundance*

*10 of Cups R
Things you haven't
told each other?
Fear of ultimate
commitment
Troubled work
environment*

*Page of Cups
Kindness and
compassion
News of a change
for the better
A job or assign-
ment that will
be fun*

*Page of Cups R
Situation that
requires thought
Stalled activity
Reactions that
are oversensitive*

*Knight of Cups
Movement
toward a goal
you feel passion
about
A new colleague
or partnership
is coming
Extending an
offer or promo-
tion*

*Knight of Cups R
Vacillating feelings
about a project
or job
Difficulty giving
to others
Living in the past*

*Queen of Cups
A nurturing,
generous col-
league or leader
A focus on
intuition
Satisfaction with
work group or
partner*

*Queen of Cups R
Wait before
reacting
Tendency toward
secrecy or self-
deception
A worrier; an over-
active imagination*

*King of Cups
Quiet power
and control
A colleague or
leader who
understands
others
A desire to help
from behind the
scenes*

*King of Cups R
A recent emotional
loss
Hidden emotions
Potential for
manipulation
of feelings*

About the Authors

Arlene Tognetti grew up in a home where religion and spiritual ideas came together. Her mother, a traditional Catholic, and her father, a more Edgar Cayce–type individual, helped her to understand that there's more to this world than what's obvious. Arlene began studying the Tarot and Astrology in the 1970s and started her own practice in 1980. She began teaching the Tarot at the University of Washington in the Experimental College in 1982, and currently teaches the Tarot at Pierce College in Tacoma. Arlene's focus is on enlightening her students and clients: "I want everyone to learn what Tarot, Astrology, and Psychic Intuition are all about and how these Intuitive Arts can help them grow and look at the choices and alternatives in their lives." Arlene is expert author, with Lisa Lenard, of *The Complete Idiot's Guide to Tarot, Second Edition*. Arlene lives in the Seattle area. Her website is www.mellinetti.com.

Deborah S. Romaine has written or co-authored more than 20 books, including *The Complete Idiot's Guide to Communicating with Spirits* with Rita S. Berkowitz, *The Complete Idiot's Guide to the Kama Sutra* with Johanina Wikoff, Ph.D., and *Thyroid Balance* with Glenn S. Rothfeld, M.D., MAc. She lives in Tacoma, Washington.

Amaranth Illuminare is a leading book producer, developing New Age and holistic wellness books for mainstream readers. Amaranth's goal: touch readers' lives. In addition to the Intuitive Arts series, Amaranth has developed many books, including *Empowering Your Life with Joy* by Gary McClain, Ph.D., and Eve Adamson; *Releasing the Goddess Within* by Gail Carr Feldman, Ph.D., and Katherine A. Gleason; and *Menu for Life: African Americans Get Healthy, Eat Well, Lose Weight, and Live Beautifully* by Otelio Randall, M.D., and Donna Randall. Amaranth's founder and creative director, Lee Ann Chearney, is the author of *Visits: Caring for an Aging Parent* and editor of *The Quotable Angel*.

The Intuitive Arts series

Use Astrology, Tarot, and Psychic Intuition to See Your Future

Discover how you can combine the Intuitive Arts to find answers to questions of daily living, use tools to help you see and make changes in your future, claim your brightest destiny, and fulfill your essential nature.

ISBN: 1-59257-106-9

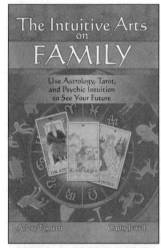

ISBN: 1-59257-110-7

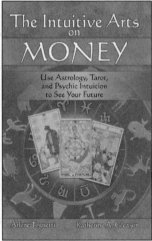

ISBN: 1-59257-107-7

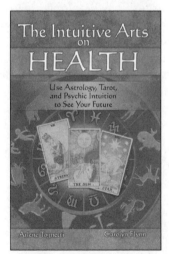

ISBN: 1-59257-109-3

ALPHA

A member of Penguin Group (USA) Inc.